# A FEW GOOD MEN

## Inspiring Biblical heroes for today's Christian men

by Richard Coekin

For my Dad, my brother and my sons, Rupert and Jonny.
*'Be on your guard; stand firm in the faith; be men of courage;*
*be strong. Do everything in love.'* **1 Corinthians 16 v 13**

A Few Good Men
© Richard Coekin/The Good Book Company 2008

Published by The Good Book Company
Elm House, 37 Elm Road, New Malden, Surrey KT3 3HB, UK.
Tel: 0845-225-0880
Fax: 0845-225-0990
email: admin@thegoodbook.co.uk

ISBN: 9781905564590

Cover design by Steve Devane

Printed in the UK by CPD

# CONTENTS

# INTRODUCTION

What kind of men do we want to be? Rugged sportsmen, smooth film stars and wild rock musicians all compete for our admiration. But are David Beckham or Shane Warne good role models for Christian men? Are Russell Crowe and Daniel Craig appropriate examples of Christian lifestyle? Should believers be trying to emulate Robbie Williams and Noel Gallagher, even if they are celebrity icons?

In the Bible, God has included dramatic accounts of how he transformed the lives of ordinary men like us to become good men, worthy of our admiration. These challenging stories both inspire us with their heroic examples and help us better understand the perfect man, Jesus Christ our Lord.

In this book I've selected 'a few good men'. Inevitably, my choice is rather subjective. I've chosen men who faced the same sorts of struggles that we often face today: immoral culture, costly decisions, sexual temptation, wealth and status, powerful opposition, sin and guilt, peer pressure, pluralistic unbelief, worry and fear.

In each case I've included both the biblical account and a dramatised version of events to try to capture the historical realities which these men faced. This certainly doesn't dare to supplement God's Word (which is entirely sufficient as it is). It is just to help us in our distracted weakness to take the biblical accounts more seriously as real events. I have also included some *Questions for Group Discussion* to help church groups engage with the implications of each chapter for our lives.

The title *A Few Good Men* comes from the Broadway play by Aaron Sorkin, which was released as a popular film in 1992 starring Tom Cruise, Jack Nicholson and Demi Moore. The film concerns a conspiracy in the US Marines that emerges from a court martial for murder, and reveals a few good men. The title seems especially appropriate for this book of biblical heroes.

Of course, only God is perfectly good, but the Bible does provide us with these stirring examples of men who climbed above being average to challenge us to do something heroic for God with our own lives. The film's most famous line, 'You can't handle the truth!' is perhaps an appropriate challenge for Christian men reading their stories today.

But after considering 'a few good men' from Bible history, it is vital to end with a chapter on Jesus Christ, the only perfect Man. It is very striking that all the best qualities that we find developed by God in the other men are most impressively perfected and combined in Jesus, to whom all the other men point. *A Few Good Men* aims to drive us to better appreciate and worship Jesus. He is the hero of this book. May *A Few Good Men* inspire and challenge us to follow Him.

# OBEDIENT NOAH

*'Noah did everything just as God commanded him'*

GENESIS 6 v 22

Obedience is not a quality much prized in modern Western culture. We rather admire the rebellious spirit, the wild man, the rogue maverick. Indeed, God did not create men to be spineless.

But God does instruct men to be obedient to those in authority over them. There is nothing pathetic about this. It is the brave obedience of the soldier to his officer's command to charge a bunker. It is the sacrificial obedience of the sportsman to his captain's appeal to put his body on the line. It is the willing obedience of the employee to his manager's instructions to get the job done.

And the Bible particularly commends submissive obedience to God. Obedience to Him, in worshipful recognition of His supreme authority, is very highly valued by God. Such obedience is impressively demonstrated for us in the dramatic ancient account of Noah.

This is the account of Noah.

Noah was a righteous man, blameless among the people of his time, and he walked with God. Noah had three sons: Shem, Ham and Japheth.

Now the earth was corrupt in God's sight and was full of violence. God saw how corrupt the earth had become, for all the people on earth had corrupted their ways. So God said to Noah, 'I am going to put an end to all people, for the earth is filled with violence because of them. I am surely going to destroy both them and the earth. So make yourself an ark of cypress wood; make rooms in it and coat it with pitch inside and out. This is how you are to build it: The ark is to be 450 feet long, 75 feet wide and 45 feet high. Make a roof for it and finish the ark to within 18 inches of the top. Put a door in the side of the ark and make lower, middle and upper decks. I am going to bring floodwaters on the earth to destroy all life under the heavens, every creature that has the breath of life in it. Everything on earth will perish. But I will establish my covenant with you, and you will enter the ark – you and your sons and your wife and your sons' wives with you. You are to bring into the ark two of all living creatures, male and female, to keep them alive with you. Two of every kind of bird, of every kind of animal and of every kind of creature that moves along the ground will come to you to be kept alive. You are to take every kind of food that is to be eaten and store it away as food for you and for them.

*Noah did everything just as God commanded him.*

The Lord then said to Noah, 'Go into the ark, you and your whole family, because I have found you righteous in this generation.'

**Genesis 6 v 9 – 7 v 1**

*From the deck of his giant ark-boat, Noah gazed out in red-eyed anguish over still waters. He searched vainly for survivors among the debris. After the savage fury of the storm floods, the all-conquering ocean seemed to recline in triumph under clear skies, gorged from swallowing the world. The rhythmic lapping of waves against the ark was punctuated by a strange knocking. Looking down to the waterline, Noah could see yet another body, this time of a small child. Face down and tangled up in wreckage, it bumped against the boat. Again he broke down sobbing, unable to process the scale of this devastation.*

*As far as the eye could see in all directions was the lifeless carnage of a civilisation. A thick primeval soup of churned-up vegetation, household effects and bloated carcasses, animal and human alike, swilled around the gently rocking ark. Noah's wife,* and soon his three sons and their wives, emerged to join him on deck. All were silenced in shock by the utterly dreadful scene. But they were also grateful, to Noah and to God. They now knew that without this crazy zoo-lifeboat, they too would be floating among the dead. After a decade of criticism, the old man had been proved right after all.

Noah had for many years been known as a righteous man, devoted to God and to others. He had been respected throughout the region for his blameless moral integrity. He walked closely with God in prayerful dependence.

But Noah was very different from the increasingly corrupt world in which he lived. The beautiful paradise that God had created had become disfigured by the violent selfishness of man. Even the animals and plant life had been dragged down into this aggressive competition. The whole creation had been gradually disintegrating and decaying. Noah had tried to call men back to the righteousness of their Maker. But he had been mocked, opposed and eventually ignored. God could plainly see that what He'd created to be so very good was now utterly spoiled by human corruption.

Noah could still recall that dreadful day when God warned of His judgment. 'I am going to put an end to all people,' He said. As mankind had disfigured God's world, God would disfigure mankind and justice would be done. But in mercy, God also promised Noah a means of escape. He told him to build the biggest wooden tub he had ever heard of. He was very specific about the dimensions, to ensure that it would be seaworthy and large enough for a huge cargo. God had then repeated His terrifying verdict upon all living things: 'Everything on earth will perish.' But again with tender kindness, God also confirmed His 'covenant', His commitment to save Noah from the coming flood, so long as Noah was obedient in building the ark.

This wooden lifeboat would be immense. It had to have three decks and enough storage for food to sustain a whole zoo of creatures for a year. This was to be home not only for Noah's family ,but also for every kind of animal and bird. God was going to completely renew His creation. Taking the world back to the watery chaos of creation, God intended to start again. He would repopulate His world with a rescued and righteous family.

As Noah pondered God's words, he realised that he and his wife would then be like Adam and Eve. Their ark would be like a miniature creation, though incredibly difficult to live in. And one day, Noah and his wife would be released into a renewed creation to be God's image, ruling over the animals and harnessing the resources of the new earth to the glory of God once more.

So Noah obeyed and did what God commanded. God had spoken plainly and would never lie. Noah couldn't ignore the way of escape designed by God for his family.

But building the enormous pitch-covered tub was extremely costly. When he explained God's promise to the family, they were shocked and cynical. In the rocky inland waste where they lived, a flood seemed quite impossible. Famine, fire, plague – perhaps. But not an immense flood in the middle of a desert! And surely God could never be so angry. 'We aren't that bad', they insisted. The family were worried. Perhaps Noah was finally going senile. He was, after all, 600 years old.

But Noah resolutely launched his extraordinary boat-building project. When he revealed the immense amount of timber involved and the scale of construction necessary, there was a terrible row in Noah's kitchen. The family business would be ruined. It could take years to fell the timber in the forests, plane and treat it and transport it back to the building site. But Noah was adamant. And they began to build.

Friends and neighbours were initially fascinated. But when Noah tried to warn them of a terrible flood to come, some were amused, but most were irritated. Some accused Noah of frightening their children and alarming the town. 'God is love. He would never destroy His own creation', they said. It was scaremongering of a fanatical kind. Noah was soon forbidden by the magistrates from speaking about God's wrath in public.

Soon the friends stopped coming. They were bored and annoyed by his depressing fundamentalism. There were plenty of preachers with a more positive message. The tourists still came, however, to see 'Noah's Folly', the monstrous boat being built in the desert by a religious nut. Noah's wife tried to stay loyal. The sons and their wives anxiously watched their inheritance being squandered on this ridiculous spiritual whim.

Of particular interest to passers-by was the growing menagerie of exotic animals and birds that Noah began to assemble (as well as the large vegetable farm he developed to feed them). This extraordinary collection of species required a great number of hired hands, which further drained the family savings. Soon there was no longer time for a holiday or money even for modest pleasures. The sons became angry and their mother despaired. Noah was ruining the family. Close friends wrote to her solemnly suggesting that she leave him. His bizarre faith in a vengeful God was destroying her life. She deserved better. But over the years of their marriage, she'd learnt to respect Noah's integrity. She stood by him, though poverty beckoned.

After several years, the huge wooden craft was finally finished. When the last scaffolding was pulled away and the fixtures and fittings installed, it sat in the large stony paddock like a giant breadbasket, baking in the sun. Or, perhaps, more like a beached whale.

Then God had spoken again: 'Go into the ark, you and your whole family, because I have found you righteous in this generation.' Apparently, faithful obedience to God's Word had made Noah acceptable. He knew he was sinful. He couldn't imagine how God could regard him as 'righteous'. But if obedience meant survival, he wasn't about to argue.

They'd immediately initiated the complex boarding programme. The different species were loaded in careful sequence to minimise handling problems. The rhinos were especially difficult to manage up the ramps. Once all the animals were loaded, the exhausting feeding and manure-disposal duties began.

The whole scenario was now totally bizarre. Cramped in their stifling and ridiculous zoo-barge, Noah and his family just waited. When they walked out on the upper deck for fresh air, passing locals would urge them to see sense, and Noah would plead with them to come aboard. It was all painfully embarrassing. Noah now spent his spare time alone, the rest of the family too weary and bitter to talk to him. Thoughts tumbled around his mind as he prayed. He had invested everything in obeying God's commands. Was he mad after all?

And then, one day, it began to rain, heavily. And it didn't stop for a month. Storm clouds blocked out the sun and torrents of water soon began to gush incessantly from every crevasse and gully.

A passing crowd of wedding guests in covered carriages had waved cheerily at them and joked about joining them if the rain ever stopped. But as the water settled in pools and then a lake washed over the ground, an eerie silence had descended. As the waters rose yet further, the family often gathered anxiously on the deck to vainly peer into the leaden gloom for signs of life. But the floodwaters just kept rising, soon above the bushes and then the trees.

One day, three weeks after the rains started, the ark itself skewed sideways, borne up on the waters. The family rushed anxiously around the lurching hull, attending to small leaks. But the construction was sound and the enormous craft floated free. Having been particularly noisy while the rain had been falling, the animals fell quiet that day. They sensed that their destiny now lay with the ark.

And then they saw terrible things. At first it was just tangled debris. But soon it was bodies. Countless bodies. Initially horrified and sometimes sick, each of the family soon subsided into a cauterised shock. Noah was inwardly crushed by the severity of God's holiness. His incredulous wife and sons whispered tormented queries about God and the future. It was one thing to believe in God's judgment; it was quite another to watch it. Noah talked quietly with them of God's burning purity that must destroy sin, of the deluded pride of rebellious mankind, and of God's mercy that offers deliverance. They listened now.

Soon the waters bore the ark above all trees and hills, and they floated high above the world. They knew they were the only survivors of God's consuming judgment. No longer was the family divided. Morning and evening, Noah gathered his family for prayer. God had done exactly what He had warned but no one had listened. He had punished the sin of the world. He had rescued His righteous family. He had purified His creation.

He was frighteningly awesome.

And then it stopped raining and the storm clouds dissolved. Noah and his family now humbly waited. Never again would they doubt God's words. Never again would they underestimate the seriousness of their sin. Never again would they resent the costs of deliverance. They now understood that only those reckoned righteous by God could hope to live in His new creation.

But what a wonderful world this would be! With all the animal species preserved and the plants soon recovering, this godly family could transport into it the lessons and skills of civilisation, and the world would go forward in righteousness.

As Noah stood upright to return to his duties within the ark, he was overcome with a sense of relief. At least he had rescued his family. He'd honestly tried to persuade those who had drowned but they just wouldn't listen. And now he understood his role in the world as the life that God preserved: obedience to God's commands.

*The animals went in two by two,*
*Hoorah, hoorah,*
*The animals went in two by two,*
*Hoorah, hoorah,*
*The animals went in two by two,*
*The elephant and the kangaroo,*
*And they all went into the ark,*
*For to get out of the rain.*

It's a catchy children's song. The account of Noah's ark, the float-ing zoo with Mr and Mrs Noah smiling under a pretty rainbow, ranks with the Christmas story as an all-time children's story-book favourite.

Which is rather sick really.

Because the account of the great flood describes a human and ecological tragedy on a scale that makes the south-east Asian Boxing Day tsunami look like a puddle in the road. Whether the universal language refers to the whole planet or the whole region, every living thing except Noah's family drowned. Men, women, little children, the sick and elderly – everyone, everywhere died.

The historicity of the biblical record is confirmed by various ancient Mesopotamian legends about a cataclysmic deluge. Those myths explain the flood as the petulant irritation of the gods at the noisiness of humanity. But the biblical record emphasises the wrath of God against sin, the mercy of God towards those with obedient faith and the commitment of God to renew His disfig-ured creation.

This is serious! Men and their families who want to survive the coming flood of God's wrath to enjoy His renewed creation through Christ must learn from Noah 'the obedience of faith' by which we are saved.

## God saw that Noah was righteous (6 v 9; 7 v 1)

We're told twice that Noah was righteous. In 6 v 9 we're told that he was 'righteous' in moral behaviour, 'blameless' in his community, and that he 'walked with God' in personal devotion. Not that he was sinless. He later sinned disgracefully. But in general, his lifestyle was marked by righteous obedience to God.

In 7 v 1 we're also told that God 'found' (literally *'saw'*) him as righteous. This contrasts with the wickedness God 'saw' all around him (6 v 12). It probably also clarifies that, just as He does for believers today, God imputed to Noah the righteous obedience of Christ so he could qualify for deliverance from His judgment.

But the particular feature of his righteousness that the apostle Peter commends is his willingness to stand against the prevailing culture. Peter calls him 'Noah, a preacher of righteousness...' (2 Peter 2 v 5). By his lifestyle and conversation, he both commended righteousness and condemned unrighteousness around him.

To be saved for God's new creation we must be the same. We shall have to swim against the rising tide of corruption around us. We must speak and act in righteousness even when nobody listens or when mockery and persecution follow. I know a project architect who was hauled before his boss and viciously harangued for refusing to lie to clients. I know a teacher at an art college in south London who was threatened with the sack if she didn't stop speaking of Christ to the students.

Only those whose obedience of faith is distinctively righteous, like Noah's, will be saved from the flood of judgment to come. (And time and again, the testimony of new believers is that the righteous integrity of a Christian colleague or friend drew them to Jesus.) By total contrast ...

## God saw that the earth was corrupt (6 v 11-12)

The earth had become corrupted (literally: *disfigured*) through the corruption of mankind. The disintegration of the natural world is directly linked to human sin. The virulence of AIDS and tuberculosis today, the bites of spiders and tigers, and the destruction of famines and earthquakes all originate in the rebellion of our race against God. Global warming, terrorism, disease and resource inequality are not just political or even moral issues but fundamentally derive from the spiritual dislocation of mankind from God.

And God is well aware of the hidden corruption in our hearts. He sees what we get up to behind closed doors or in the deepest recesses of our ambitions. However deeply hidden we think our corruptions are, God sees it all. We often assume that the idolatry of misplaced devotion in our hearts remains undetected. We imagine that, because we've forgotten it, sin not witnessed by others or that which we've tried to correct or make up for is ignored by God. But every sin remains as permanently exposed to His gaze as the statue on top of Nelson's column in broad daylight. God sees everything! The 19th-century American novelist Mark Twain once wanted to expose the prevalence of secret sin. He reported: 'I once sent a dozen of my friends a telegram saying "Flee at once – all is discovered!" They all left town immediately.' As he wrote elsewhere: 'Everyone is a moon and has a dark side which he never shows to anybody.' But God can see the back of the moon and the bottom of our own hearts. He is blind to nothing. The account of Noah warns us that God sees and will punish all the corruptions of the human heart.

Indeed, the apostle Paul writes: 'This will take place on the day when God will judge men's secrets through Jesus Christ, as my gospel declares' (Romans 2 v 16). If a gospel talk or evening course does not warn of this judgement of secrets, it is not giving the apostolic gospel of Scripture. This is what Noah tried to warn people about. And if we are not warning people about it, we are not righteous like Noah.

So Noah was righteous but the world was corrupt. And God was about to unleash His flood of judgment. The New Testament draws four simple lessons from Noah's experience:

## God unexpectedly punished sinners! (6 v 13)
God said: 'I am going to put an end to all people.' Our holy

Creator was never going to tolerate such sustained defiance of His authority and defacing of His creation. God is love, but His love is holy love that will not ignore moral corruption and the victims of evil. He must punish sin and cleanse His creation, or He is not a good God. Peter warns: 'If he did not spare the ancient world when he brought the flood on its ungodly people ... then the Lord knows how to ... hold the unrighteous for the day of judgment, while continuing their punishment' (2 Peter 2 v 5-9). The flood demonstrates that God will punish sinners.

Moreover, the flood shows that God will judge even though people don't expect it. Jesus warned:

> As it was in the days of Noah, so it will be at the coming of the Son of Man. For in the days before the flood, people were eating and drinking, marrying and giving in marriage, up to the day Noah entered the ark; and they knew nothing about what would happen until the flood came and took them all away. That is how it will be at the coming of the Son of Man (Matthew 24 v 37-39).

Whether Jesus returns during our lifetime, or after we've died, He will come unexpectedly to raise us all to face His searching examination. Few of our family, friends and colleagues expect this, but Noah's experience proves that God will do it.

But next time God will come not in a flood, but in fire. Paul writes:

> This will happen when the Lord Jesus is revealed from heaven in blazing fire with his powerful angels. He will punish those who do not know God and do not obey the gospel of our Lord Jesus. They will be punished with everlasting destruction and shut out from the presence of the Lord and from the majesty of his power on the day he comes to be glorified in his holy people (2 Thessalonians 1 v 7-10).

It doesn't help anyone to sanitise the horror of this judgment. The graphic film footage of that 2004 earthquake and tsunami, centred off Sumatra in Indonesia, when 229,000 people died and countless towns and villages were devastated, is very sobering. One third of the victims were children, 9000 were tourists on holiday. But this is nothing like the total devastation which Noah witnessed by the hand of God when everyone died. These are hard truths to hear. But even the flood is as nothing compared to the return of Christ, when everyone who has ever lived will be judged and all unbelievers sent to hell. When Christ returns, the whole universe will be engulfed in flames:

> The day of the Lord will come like a thief. The heavens will disappear with a roar; the elements will be destroyed by fire, and the earth and everything in it will be laid bare… That day will bring about the destruction of the heavens by fire, and the elements will melt in the heat. But in keeping with his promise we are looking forward to a new heaven and a new earth, the home of righteousness. **2 Peter 3 v 10-13**

When Peter calls Noah 'a preacher of righteousness', it was not his own righteousness but God's that he preached. He proclaimed that God is both righteous to punish sin and righteous to save those who obey His message of salvation from judgment, by providing in Christ's obedience unto death the righteous life we need to live in the 'home of righteousness'.

Noah's experience emphatically demonstrates that God will keep His promise to unexpectedly punish sin. His judgment is coming. Be very afraid!

Thankfully there is more.

## God patiently provided salvation! (6 v 14-17)

God came in salvation as well as judgment. God gave Noah very specific dimensions for a lifeboat capable of saving his family and the creation in miniature. This ark foreshadowed the salvation of Moses in a pitch-covered basket in the waters of the Nile, and that of Israel through the carefully-designed tabernacle-temple for the saving presence of God.

But ultimately, the provision of the ark points to the provision of Jesus, in whose resurrection from the dead we are saved. As the ark rose up on the waters of judgment preserving all within it, so Jesus' rising up from His grave preserves all who are by faith represented in Him. The apostle Peter explores this parallel between salvation in the ark and salvation in Jesus:

> God waited patiently in the days of Noah while the ark was being built. In it only a few people, eight in all, were saved through water, and this water symbolises baptism that now saves you also – not the removal of dirt from the body but the pledge of a good conscience towards God. It saves you by the resurrection of Jesus Christ, who has gone into heaven and is at God's right hand… **1 Peter 3 v 20-22**

These are complex verses and it's helpful to break them down into simple truths:

- God waited patiently for Noah to build the ark just as He waits patiently today for His people to become Christians.
- As the floodwater was used to raise up Noah in the ark safe above God's judgment, so the waters of baptism symbolise our sharing in the raising of Jesus safe above the judgment of our sin.
- It is not washing in the water of baptism that saves anyone, 'not the removal of dirt from the body' (unbelieving adults or babies are not saved by a baptism ceremony). Rather, as Noah's faith in God's promise was how Noah was saved, so it is faith in God's gospel, 'the pledge of a good conscience towards God', that saves us in the resurrection of Jesus 'who has gone into heaven'.

Put simply, Noah obediently building and entering the ark to be saved is like Christians obediently trusting in Christ's resurrection from the dead to be saved. God gave Noah the ark. God gave us His Son.

Like Noah, we too must obey God's instructions for salvation. When I was a boy, my family moved to live in Townsville, North Queensland, for several years. In 1971, a terrible cyclone named 'Cyclone Anthea' struck the town and flattened most of it. Despite the devastation, only a couple of people died because we were all repeatedly given specific instructions on the radio about how to survive. I recall that, as the fiercest winds passed over our house, my family had to crouch together under the kitchen table which my father had dragged into the bathroom. Apparently this was the safest place to be. It all seemed great fun to the kids, but it was fairly terrifying for my parents. They would never have dreamt of ignoring the safety instructions. Lives were at stake and we obeyed happily.

So it was for Noah and so it is for Christians today. The day of wrath will be much worse than a cyclone or even a great flood. If we believe the warnings, we will obey the instructions. That is the way to survive. It's that simple.

### God faithfully kept His covenant! (6 v 18)

God's covenant with Noah was His binding commitment and solemn promise to save him. This was the first of a series of covenants that God would also announce to Abraham, Moses, David and Jeremiah. Here in Genesis 6, it was a promise to save Noah. (When it was repeated in chapter 9, it was extended to become a promise to every living creature never again to send a flood to destroy the earth. The rainbow was given as a sign or pledge reminding us of the promise.)

Noah found that, through the battering of storms and a year on the open floodwaters, God honoured His covenant.

This is enormously important for Christians today. For God has now established a new covenant with us by the blood of Jesus' death on the cross. The terms of that covenant, based upon the new forgiveness of our sins in Christ, are threefold. God grants to His people, first, His law in our hearts (the desire to obey God which every Christian has); second, that He will be our God and we will be His people (the power to please God which every Christian has); third, to know God personally (which every Christian does) (Hebrews 8). This wonderful covenant was permanently established by Jesus' death, as He explained the night before He died: 'In the same way, after supper he took the cup, saying, "This cup is the new covenant in my blood; do this, whenever you drink it, in remembrance of me"' (1 Corinthians 11 v 25).

Noah's experience was that God kept His covenant promise of salvation. He will keep His promise to us, too.

I once talked with a man who taught me what covenant commitment involves. He quietly explained that his wife was psychiatrically ill. It turned out that she had manic depression, which at its worst made her so inappropriately bold as to render her sexually promiscuous. With a heavy heart, he told me that whenever he walked into the town where he lived, he knew that lots of the men he met had slept with his wife during her manic episodes. The pain of this humiliation was nearly unbearable. But he also told me that, since he had promised on his wedding day to love her 'for better, for worse, for richer, for poorer, in sickness and in health', he would remain faithful to his marriage covenant. That's covenant commitment. That's like God's covenant commitment – faithful to His promise, despite our bad behaviour, even thought it cost Him the death of His Son.

## God generously rewarded obedience! (6 v 22 – 7 v 1)

The writer to the Hebrews describes Noah's faith in these words: '...By faith Noah, when warned about things not yet seen, in holy fear built an ark to save his family. By his faith he condemned the world and became heir of the righteousness that comes by faith' (Hebrews 11 v 7).

Noah's saving faith began with believing God's warning. He believed it even though there was no visible evidence of judgment coming. Indeed, a destructive flood seemed as implausible then as final judgment seems to us today. But real faith believes God's Word, not because it seems sensible to us (though it usually does), but because God says it. Saving faith believes God's promise of deliverance from judgment and rescue into a new world, without yet experiencing what is promised.

But this saving faith must be expressed in obedience. If God is really trusted, He will be obeyed, not just in fine sermons, songs and prayers, but in practice and at cost. Although Noah's deliverance was provided as a gift entirely by God, it was only accessed by obedience. If Noah had refused to build as God told him to, there would have been no ark to be saved in. God gave him faith to be righteous in obedience. Noah had to exercise it.

In the same way, God has provided complete salvation in Christ. But we only access it by obeying His command to rely upon Him. God gives us faith to be righteous in obedience. Paul calls this 'the obedience that comes from faith' (Romans 1 v 5). There is no assurance of salvation in Christ if there is no practical obedience to God's commands in our lives, because real faith is expressed in obedience. If we want Christ as our Saviour, we must accept Him as Lord. For He is both, and we cannot have the Saviour without having the Lord. Faith in our Saviour is expressed in obedience to our Lord.

Are we obedient? Do we obey the Ten Commandments, understood in the light of the gospel? Is our worship given to the God who has revealed himself in Christ? Are we redesigning God's image, who is Christ, in our imagination? Are we irreverent towards Him or His King in our speech? Are we reliant on His Son for our eternal rest? Do we show respect to the parents God gave us, as the Son does to the Father? Are we guilty of destructive anger while God forgives us in Jesus? Have we repented of adulterous lust because God has remained faithful in sending His Son? Do we keep money from gospel ministry, an employer or the poor while God is so generous to us in giving us His Son? Are we envious of another man's wife, house or job as if God doesn't know, or His Son understand, what we need? Jesus said: 'Whoever has my commands and obeys them, he is the one who loves me ... If anyone loves me, he will obey my teaching.' (John 14 v 21, 23). If we don't obey the law of Christ, we can't claim to love Him.

Noah's obedience was rewarded with the inheritance of Christ's righteousness that we all need in order to enter the new heavens and the new earth. God said: 'I have found you righteous' (7 v 1). This means 'I am treating you as righteous', in the same way that

He treats Christians as righteous or 'justified'. Charles Dickens' book *A Tale of Two Cities* provides a helpful analogy. The story is set in the final years of the 18th century and during the French Revolution. Two men, very similar in appearance, love the same woman. She sensibly loves the fine gentleman of the two, Charles Darnay, rather than the rat, Sidney Carton. But Darnay is captured and locked up in a dungeon in Paris, facing execution by guillotine the following day. Carton decides to do the only good thing he will ever do, for the sake of the woman he loves. With a friend, Carton goes to Darnay's jail and drugs him. While Darnay is unconscious, Carton exchanges clothes with him. The drugged Charles Darnay is then taken from the prison in Carton's clothes. With Carton's pass papers, he is taken across the barricades around Paris and back to his beloved in England. Meanwhile, Carton is guillotined in Darnay's place.

This is a tale of extraordinary love and self-sacrifice that illustrates what Christ has done for us. A simple swap took place. Carton was treated as if he were Darnay and executed so that Darnay could be treated as if he were Carton and allowed to return to England. In a similar fashion, God the Son became an ordinary man so that He could be treated like us and punished on the cross for our sin. He did this so that we can be treated as if we were Him: clothed in His righteous life and with His access to heaven, we can travel across the barricades into heaven. He was treated as if He were us (and punished) so we can be treated as if we were Him (and accepted as righteous, or 'justified'). It was this righteousness of Christ that Noah inherited. Those whose faith is, like Noah's, expressed in obedience are given the righteousness we need to enter heaven.

The Bible makes one final observation about Noah's righteousness. Because he wasn't the representative of others, his righteousness could not count for anyone else: 'If a country sins against me by being unfaithful and I stretch out my hand against it ... even if these three men – Noah, Daniel and Job – were in it, they could save only themselves by their righteousness, declares the Sovereign Lord' (Ezekiel 14 v 13-14). Noah's righteous obedience, perfected with Christ's righteousness, only counted for him. His family were saved, not by Noah, but by joining his faithful obedience (no doubt under considerable pressure from Noah!). Sadly, Noah's righteousness couldn't save anyone else of his generation. They all perished.

But Christ's righteousness is counted to all God's people because He is our representative. When David Beckham was England football captain, he often took free kicks close to goal. If he scored, the rest of the team and the England supporters at the stadium and all around the world would all yell: 'We've scored!' Only one man kicked the ball, but it counted for every England fan. Likewise, since Jesus is our captain, His righteous obedience counts for all of us in a way that Noah's could not.

### God renewed His creation

The story of Noah reveals God's commitment to restoring creation. He could have obliterated the whole world and decided that the human experiment couldn't work. But He didn't, because God is committed to a new creation in which countless brothers and sisters of Jesus praise Him for the cross and enjoy the gracious goodness of the Father forever. So God is committed to destroying and renewing His creation.

It's a bit like the US version of *Extreme Makeover* (not the UK version where husbands try to improve their wives!). In this TV series, Ty Pennington and a vast team of top designers and builders completely rebuild someone's home. It's fantastically sentimental. The team will identify a deserving family, perhaps a single-parent family with a cancer-suffering child living in a tiny dilapidated shack with no prospect of improving their home. Unannounced, the team arrive and pack the bewildered family off on holiday, and while they are away, they recruit the whole town to help rebuild the family home.

They start by completely destroying the old hovel. Then they build a wonderful mansion, designed to suit every need and dream of that particular family, and fill it with a fortune's worth of state-of-the-art audio and sports equipment, etc. The family comes back and when the bus that is blocking the view is moved out of the way to reveal the new home, the family invariably breaks down in floods of tears while the whole town cheers them on. As they are shown around their new home, they weep with joy, and the whole programme is just wonderful! Well, God is committed to a cosmic *Extreme Makeover*, with a wonderful new creation for us all to enjoy. They will be fantastic days when we are shown around our new home in heaven. The flood account is the guarantee that God will completely renovate and renew His creation.

### 'Savour the act of saving'

One last thing. Hebrews 11 says that Noah 'built an ark to save his family'. Having persuaded them to join him despite the hostility around him, imagine how relieved and satisfied he felt not just on the ark, but in the restored creation. What greater joy can there be for a man than resolutely to try to keep praying, living and teaching the Scriptures, persuading his family to take refuge in Christ?

The most famous of the coxswains of the legendary Moelfre lifeboats operating from Moelfre in Anglesey, North Wales, is Dick Evans. He won the first of his gold medals for his bravery in the rescue of the *Hindlea* in October 1959. In mountainous seas and hurricane winds, Evans ten times steered his little lifeboat under the stricken vessel so that the exhausted crew could jump onto the lifeboat. Immediately after the rescue Evans reported: 'I sat on the slipway utterly exhausted. Suddenly I realised that tears were streaming down my face. They were tears of joy. My crew and I have saved eight men from a certain death and I felt very happy about it.' I'm sure he did. And I imagine Noah felt similarly about his own family, and we will about ours if we can sit on the shores of heaven and know that we've spent our lives saving people too.

Noah teaches us the wisdom of obedience. His story teaches us that God will always keep His word: He punished sinners, He provided salvation, He kept his covenant and He rewarded obedience. He destroyed and renewed His creation (which is linked to the future death and resurrection of His Son). Above all, Noah teaches men to express their confidence in God with practical, active obedience. If he could obey God by building an ark, then we can obey the more obvious instructions of God's Word. For this, he plainly ranks among 'a few good men'.

## BIBLE BACKGROUND

### *The Bible*

Scripture is God's compilation of Spirit-directed books that progressively reveal God's gospel: that Jesus (the crucified Nazarene) is Christ (the promised Saviour-King) our Lord (our divine, risen Ruler and returning Judge). Genesis begins the message with an account of creation and of the origins of Israel and the Saviour.

### *Genesis*

Genesis is a series of ten carefully-constructed accounts of the descendants of key characters, grouped in four principal sections:

• Chapters 1-11 explain why the world needs God's Saviour. God created the heavens and the earth by His word, with mankind as His image to rule creation, enjoying the blessings of God's eternal rest. When man rebelled against God, he was expelled from God's paradise kingdom and condemned to death.

• Thereafter we discover from the life of Abraham (ch 12-22) that God is faithful to His promise of an inheritance in the kingdom of God.

• We learn from the life of Jacob (ch 25-35) that God is gracious to sinners.

• We then learn from the life of Joseph (ch 37-50) that God is sovereign to save His people through His servant.

### *Noah*

The account of Noah concerns the great flood when Noah was 600 years old.

It occupies a whole section (ch 6-9) midway between Adam and Abraham, in the section explaining the world's need of a Saviour. The tale of Noah's rescue from the flood in an ark-boat establishes that God is grieved by sin and will punish sinners; that God provides salvation for His people; that He keeps His covenant promises; that He rewards those who express their faith in righteous obedience; and that God is committed to destroying and renewing His disfigured creation.

### *The New Testament*

New Testament writers see these accounts as parallel to the situation of Christians today. Like Noah, we must believe God's warning of future judgment, obey His instructions for salvation in Christ, trust His covenant commitment to save us and look forward to life in the renewed creation when it comes with Christ.

## Questions for group discussion

1. Why do we find it hard to believe that God will come in judgment one day?

2. How can we express our faith in God by obedience?

3. When do we doubt that God will save us?

4. What are the implications of knowing that God will destroy and renew His creation?

# 2 SACRIFICIAL ABRAHAM

*'Now I know that you fear God, because
you have not withheld from me your son'*

GENESIS 22 v12

S acrifice is still rightly honoured in western society. The sacrifices made by the armed forces, by police, ambulance and fire services, by ordinary citizens who give themselves to serve in local charities, schools and hospitals, are admired by most people. Pre-eminent, perhaps, in recent times was the supreme sacrifice made by 343 of the firemen and paramedics of the New York Fire Department in trying to rescue those trapped in the burning 'Twin Towers' of the World Trade Centre on 9/11, that tragic day in world history.

At 'Ground Zero' today, visitors can still see pictures of those fire officers. They returned time and again into those buildings alight with burning jet fuel to rescue people, before losing their own lives when the buildings collapsed. Such sacrifice is an expression of commitment and love.

God has expressed His love for us in self-sacrifice, accepting the penalty for our sin on the cross. He likewise appreciates our expression of love for Him in self-sacrifice. Indeed, this is how we 'worship' Him: 'Therefore, I urge you, brothers, in view of God's mercy, to offer your bodies as living sacrifices, holy and pleasing to God – this is your spiritual [appropriate] act of worship' (Romans 12 v 1). One of the greatest sacrifices of worship made in Scripture was that of Abraham, our great ancestor in faith:

Some time later God tested Abraham. He said to him, 'Abraham!'

'Here I am,' he replied.

Then God said, 'Take your son, your only son, Isaac, whom you love, and go to the region of Moriah. Sacrifice him there as a burnt offering on one of the mountains I will tell you about.'

Early the next morning Abraham got up and saddled his donkey. He took with him two of his servants and his son Isaac. When he had cut enough wood for the burnt offering, he set out for the place God had told him about. On the third day Abraham looked up and saw the place in the distance. He said to his servants, 'Stay here with the donkey while I and the boy go over there. We will worship and then we will come back to you.'

Abraham took the wood for the burnt offering and placed it on his son Isaac, and he himself carried the fire and the knife. As the two of them went on together, Isaac spoke up and said to his father Abraham, 'Father?'

'Yes, my son?' Abraham replied.

'The fire and wood are here,' Isaac said, 'but where is the lamb for the burnt offering?'

Abraham answered, 'God himself will provide the lamb for the burnt offering, my son.' And the two of them went on together.

When they reached the place God had told him about, Abraham built an altar there and arranged the wood on it. He bound his son Isaac and laid him on the altar, on top of the wood. Then he reached out his hand and took the knife to slay his son. But the angel of the LORD called out to him from heaven, 'Abraham! Abraham!'

'Here I am,' he replied.

'Do not lay a hand on the boy,' he said. 'Do not do anything to him. Now I know that you fear God, because you have not withheld from me your son, your only son.'

Abraham looked up and there in a thicket he saw a ram caught by its horns. He went over and took the ram and sacrificed it as a burnt offering instead of his son. So Abraham called that place The LORD Will Provide. And to this day it is said, 'On the mountain of the LORD it will be provided.'

The angel of the LORD called to Abraham from heaven a second time and said, 'I swear by myself, declares the LORD, that because you have done this and have not withheld your son, your only son, I will surely bless you and make your descendants as numerous as the stars in the sky and as the sand on the seashore. Your descendants will take possession of the cities of their enemies, and through your offspring all nations on earth will be blessed, because you have obeyed me.'

Then Abraham returned to his servants, and they set off together for Beersheba. And Abraham stayed in Beersheba.

**Genesis 22 v 1-19**

*The old man and his teenage son staggered the last few metres up the hill, short of breath and with aching limbs. Abraham was carrying a clay pot of fire and Isaac a large stack of firewood on his back. But even as they collapsed at the summit and gathered their strength, neither was able to speak. Abraham was weeping quietly into his beard, trying to hide his anguished face from the anxious eyes of his son. As they gazed south from Mount Moriah, back across the beautiful Kidron valley towards Beersheba from where they'd come, they could make out the little campsite, servants and tethered donkey they'd left at the bottom of the hill. This traumatic end to their journey had to be undertaken alone.*

*Three days earlier, the LORD had called to Abraham once more. Abraham had failed the LORD too many times before, and he welcomed this chance to respond well. 'Here I am,' he'd replied, submissive and eager to obey. The LORD had been so good to him over the years. Back in Haran, God had promised Abraham and his descendants a new kingdom that would become a blessing to all peoples on earth, as the Garden of Eden had once been. As promised, God had brought him to this beautiful land. He'd showered him with blessings. And even though his wife Sarah was barren for so many years, He had given them a miracle baby* in their old age. Isaac was a young man now, the apple of his mother's eye and the focus of all God's promises for the future.

Until three days ago. God had said: 'Take your son, your only son, Isaac, whom you love, and go to the region of Moriah. Sacrifice him there as a burnt offering ...' Of course, Abraham was utterly devastated. What God was asking seemed incomprehensible – indeed, morally disgusting. The LORD is holy! He could not approve of child sacrifice such as pagan tribes practised. Even if this son was the LORD's to give and the LORD's to take away, how could it be right to order Abraham to kill his own son?

And it was totally illogical – this was the very son through whom God had promised to give a great nation of descendants! Having miraculously given him life in Sarah's barren womb, it was outrageous now to kill him.

And it seemed so cruel. This was their special, only son. God knew how intensely he and Sarah had longed for a child. He knew how they now adored Isaac. It seemed, frankly, sadistic to expect Abraham to sacrifice him. None of it made any sense. Sarah had naturally been inconsolable in her grief. After the distraught raging and shouting, she'd just collapsed in a chair staring into the distance in a traumatised daze.

But as Abraham lay in bed that night, desperate thoughts tumbling around in the confusion of his mind, a few simple things had become clear. Over the years, he'd learnt that the LORD always keeps His promises, however impossible they seem. He'd learnt that he was just too small to try to grasp the LORD's great designs. He'd learnt to trust Him. But this was an incredible thing that the LORD was asking. He couldn't bear to think of actually tying Isaac to an altar to kill him. How could he possibly cremate his own son?

And then it had dawned on him. God had clearly promised a nation of descendants from Isaac. Since God had now equally clearly commanded Abraham to sacrifice him as a burnt offering, then, somehow, God would have to raise him from the dead! Nothing else would fulfil both the promise and the command.

*God had never been cruel. Quite the opposite – He was some-
times frightening and often inscrutable, but He was always gracious. Impossible though it sounded, Abraham concluded that the
LORD would have to raise Isaac from the dead. He'd seen God's
power give life to Sarah's dead womb. Presumably He was planning to give life again. There was no other way of reconciling
what he knew of God with this command. Eventually, too
exhausted to think any more, he fell asleep with nowhere else to
go. He couldn't disobey a direct order from God. He would have
to trust the LORD to do the right thing. Though it still seemed barbaric to Abraham.*

*And so, just as when the LORD first called Abraham to go to this
land, so now, at the end of his life, Abraham obeyed and went.
Early in the morning, so as to obey promptly, he saddled the donkey and awakened two of the servants. He got Isaac up, and after
cutting plenty of good wood for the sacrifice, began the 80-kilo-
metre journey to Moriah.*

*As they walked, Isaac soon realised that something was very
wrong. His father hardly uttered a word and from time to time
broke down into fits of uncontrollable sobbing. Abraham was
frantically trying to remain resolute. Many times, he almost
turned back as rebellion and anger welled up in his heart towards
God. Again and again, he restrained himself, remembering the
merciful character of the LORD. God must know what He was
doing. As always, the LORD would want his trust. It was through
such faith in God's gospel promise that he'd first been declared
acceptable to God. That same faith was required again now. He
hardly slept or ate for the entire three days. When they arrived at
Moriah, he summoned all his confidence in the LORD to declare to
his servants what he now understood they were doing: 'Stay here
with the donkey while I and the boy go over there. We will worship and then we will come back to you.'*

*As they'd plodded up the mountain track, he'd gone over those
words again and again: 'We will worship ... we will worship ... we*

will worship.' He was determined to worship the LORD in reverent obedience. He could only do this thing for God. 'We will come back ... we will come back ... we will come back.' He would surely return with Isaac resurrected somehow from the dead. It was the only sensible explanation.

Dear Isaac had very nearly broken his heart. He had quietly asked, 'Father ... where is the lamb for the burnt offering?' Abraham had weakly replied: 'God Himself will provide the lamb for the burnt offering, my son.' He'd hoped to hide the truth from Isaac a little longer. But, as always, Isaac knew exactly what was going on. He knew he was the special gift from God. Abraham could see in Isaac's eyes that he knew that he was the sacrifice. Abraham's faith in the LORD was being tested to the absolute limit. He was now too weary to know how to feel. At the top of the hill, when his panting abated, Abraham faced the awful moment of truth. It was time.

Feeling sick, Abraham took the firewood and arranged it carefully upon a flat outcrop of rock. He turned to embrace his son for the last time. They wept uncontrollably, feeble old father and strapping young man. Isaac then stood submissively as Abraham, weak and trembling, bound him with cords and simple knots. Isaac then sat on the altar and lay down meekly. Abraham loved this boy more than life itself. But the LORD had commanded.

Abraham stood over him for a few moments, desperately trying to pray, tears streaming down his face. Father and son then searched each other's face briefly and Abraham raised the flint knife high over the boy, ready to strike. In his heart he cried out to the LORD, 'To worship ... and to come back', and then made to plunge the dagger into his son's heart.

'Abraham!' came the sudden, heavenly call once more. 'Abraham!' He checked his downward arc. 'Here I am,' he replied once again. 'Do not lay a hand on the boy. Now I know that you fear God, because you have not withheld from me your son, your only son.'

After a few moments of frozen incomprehension, Abraham began furiously untying Isaac from his bonds and dragged him from the altar. Overwhelmed with excitement, the two fell to the ground in a heap. Relief, then laughter and eventually tears of joy flooded over them. Abraham had been right to trust the LORD. God would never abandon His promises. God had clearly been testing and strengthening his faith – helping him to trust the LORD whatever it cost. Abraham uttered a brief, confused prayer of thanks to God, fearful of hearing another word.

Rising to their feet, they saw a ram caught by its horns in a thicket nearby. It now seemed obvious. The LORD was indeed providing the sacrifice, a substitute for Isaac. Resolutely, Isaac gripped the struggling sheep, while Abraham slashed its throat with the dagger meant for Isaac. As the animal fell limp and the blood gushed over the wool, this death seemed strangely welcome to them both. They piled the sheep onto the altar, not minding the bloodstains on their clothing, and lit the fire. Arm in arm, as the fire crackled around the carcass and the smoke rose high in the sky towards heaven, father and son now solemnly took turns to thank the LORD for providing that sacrifice. And then they fell silent, watching the fire and trying to grasp what it all meant.

Once more the voice of the LORD pierced the silence, and Abraham and Isaac fell to their knees as they listened, gazing into the heavens. 'Because you have done this and have not withheld your son, your only son, I will surely bless you and make your descendants as numerous as the stars in the sky and as the sand on the seashore. Through your offspring all nations on earth will be blessed, because you have obeyed me.'

After the LORD had finished speaking, and once the flames of sacrifice were dying down to embers, Abraham and Isaac turned to leave. 'We need to get back to tell Mother,' said Isaac. 'She'll be frantic.'

*'Yes, she will,' replied Abraham. 'But we also have some urgent work to do,' added the old man, with laughter in his eyes. 'If you're going to have all these descendants ... we'd better find you a wife!' And they roared and howled and cackled with laughter, all the way back to Beersheba.*

*Abraham, Sarah and Isaac had learnt in the most dramatic way imaginable that faith in the LORD must be sacrificial faith, willing to give up anything in obedience to God, trusting that He knows what is best. Saving faith must be sacrificial.*

————

Today in Jerusalem, within the Muslim 'Dome of the Rock' built upon the site of Solomon's temple in AD 691, lies an exposed slab of rock. It is supposed to be the place where Abraham was willing to sacrifice his son. Pilgrims file past it daily in reverence. Muslims celebrate this event in their feast of Eid ul-Adha (the Feast of Sacrifice) – though they believe the son involved was Ishmael. Jews still celebrate the 'binding of Isaac' (though the repetition of Abraham's name in verses 1 and 15 emphasises that it is Abraham's faith and not Isaac's submissiveness which is being commended here). And Christians regard this monumental exercise of sacrificial faith as a model of faith in the gospel promise.

After reading of the Creator's judgement of sin in Genesis 1-11, we are shown in Genesis 12-25 that Abraham's faith in God's gospel promise was the way of salvation from that judgment. The account of Abraham begins and ends with him obeying a command to 'go'. In chapter 12 he was told to 'go' to the land God would show him (the earthly kingdom of God). In chapter 22, in the climax to his life of faith, he was told to 'go' to the region of Moriah (to sacrifice what was most precious to him). Christian faith is likewise fundamentally about obeying God's command to leave this world for a life in the kingdom of God, ready to sacrifice anything for the LORD as we go.

## God tested Abraham (v 1-2)

Readers are told in verses 1-2 something which Abraham was not told. This command was not a desire for child sacrifice but a 'test' of Abraham's faith. While Satan 'tests' (tempts) our faith in God's Word to try to get us to abandon it, the LORD only tests our faith to purify and strengthen it, as gold is refined in a furnace. What God requires of us in His Word may sometimes be deeply perplexing and extremely costly. Like Abraham, we must learn to trust Him. When Abraham heard the call of God, he responded with the willing submission of Samuel, David and Isaiah (applied to Jesus in Hebrews 10): 'Here I am.'

But then came the astonishing command: 'Take your son, your only son, Isaac, whom you love … Sacrifice him there as a burnt offering.' The word 'son' is used repeatedly as the key word of the whole passage, emphasising the immense sacrifice involved.

Mount Moriah was the very hill on which Jerusalem and the temple would later be built. The provision of a substitutionary sacrifice for Isaac foreshadows not only the animal sacrifices of the temple, but also the ultimate sacrifice of Christ on the cross. There are four aspects to this foreshadowing.

First, the journey up the hill looked forward not only to Israel's journey up Mount Sinai to sacrifice, but also to Christ's ascent to His cross, carrying not firewood but the wooden beam to which He would be nailed.

Second, the provision of a sheep for sacrifice prefigured not only the Passover lambs that would later die to satisfy the LORD when He 'passed over' Israel in His judgment upon Egypt; it also prefigured Jesus, the 'Lamb of God who takes away the sin of the world'. Jesus would be the ultimate 'Passover' sacrifice, who swapped places with the sons of God to suffer our penalty for us.

Third, Abraham's willingness to sacrifice his beloved son, rewarded by receiving him back as if from the dead, foreshadowed the love of God. As we contemplate the horror of it, we begin to grasp better what our Father in heaven did at the cross – giving His precious Son to suffer a brutal death and the spiritual torture of hell for us, before receiving Him back from the dead. Such is His amazing love for us.

And fourth, as the sacrificial lamb offered here secured the covenant promise to Abraham of many descendants to come, so Christ's sacrificial death secured for all believers the blessings of the New Covenant, based upon the forgiveness of our sins. As Abraham was confirmed by his faithful offering to be the ancestor of countless descendants, so Jesus was confirmed by His self-sacrifice to be the founder of the new humanity of forgiven people. The whole episode at Mount Moriah was given that we may better appreciate what was achieved by the death of Christ.

But there are three particular aspects of Abraham's faith to which the New Testament draws attention. They emerge from the three stages of his epic journey.

### 1. Abraham believed that God could raise the dead! (v 3-5)
When Abraham said to the servants: 'We will worship and then we will come back to you', he had clearly realised that God was well able to raise Isaac from the dead in order to keep His promise about Isaac's descendants. This helps explain how Abraham ever managed actually to raise the knife to slay his own son! In Hebrews we read:

> By faith Abraham, when God tested him, offered Isaac as a sacrifice. He who had received the promises was about to sacrifice his one and only son, even though God had said to him:
>
> 'It is through Isaac that your offspring will be reckoned.' Abraham reasoned that God could raise the dead, and figuratively speaking, he did receive Isaac back from death. **Hebrews 11 v 17-19**

The faith of Abraham, saving faith, reasons that God will raise the dead. This is actually the same faith that is required of all Christians (indeed, Hebrews 11 describes not especially heroic faith but the faith of all believers). We all believe that God has raised His own Son from the dead and that He will do the same for us. Although this is not the most remarkable aspect of Abraham's faith, though he did come to his conclusion without the evidence of Jesus' resurrection to support it. All Christians believe that God has and will raise the dead. This is why Christians are prepared to die for Christ and to let members of their families die for him as well.

In *Killing Fields, Living Fields,* a moving account of the Christian church in Cambodia during the horrific oppression of the Khmer Rouge under Pol Pot in the 1970s, Don Cormack describes one of the many executions of a Christian family, led by a man called Haim. The faith of this family reveals the same confidence in resurrection life that Abraham displayed:

> A sickly smell of death hung in the air. Curious villagers foraging in the scrub nearby lingered, half hidden, watching the familiar routine as the family were ordered to dig a large grave for themselves. Then, consenting to Haim's request for a moment to prepare themselves for death, father, mother, and children, hands linked, knelt together around the gaping pit. With loud cries to God, Haim began exhorting both the Khmer Rouge and all those looking on from afar to repent and believe the gospel. Then in panic, one of Haim's young sons leapt to his feet, bolted into the surrounding bush and disappeared. Haim jumped up and with amazing coolness and authority prevailed upon the Khmer Rouge not to pursue the lad, but to allow him to call the boy back. The knots of onlookers, peering around trees, the Khmer Rouge, and the stunned family still kneeling at the graveside, looked on in awe as Haim began calling his son, pleading with him to return and die together with his family. 'What comparison, my son,' he called out, 'stealing a few more days of life in the wilderness, a fugitive, wretched and alone, to joining your family here momentarily around this grave but soon around the throne of God, free forever in Paradise?' After a few tense minutes the bushes parted, and the lad, weeping, walked slowly back to his place with the kneeling family. 'Now we are ready to go,' said Haim to the Khmer Rouge.' [1]

The family were all killed, their bodies toppling into the grave, but their souls released into the presence of Jesus forever, awaiting the resurrection of their bodies.

That is the faith of Abraham, faith in God's power to raise the dead. It is normal Christian faith. We believe that God has raised Jesus from the dead. We believe that, by faith in Him, all believers share in His resurrection from the dead. This means we have already been judged, justified and accepted into heaven in our representative, Jesus. We experience this new resurrection life within us. We believe that one day, when Christ returns to destroy and resurrect creation, we shall be bodily raised with it. And if, tragically, it ever came to offering our own lives or the lives of those we love for God, we could do so in confidence that God will raise us and them to life. In this faith, Christians may contend for the faith, return home to persecution or travel as missionaries into hostile cultures or the threat of disease, knowing that even if we must sacrifice our lives, God will raise us to life with Him. Abraham demonstrated faith that God can raise the dead.

However, the more remarkable aspect of Abraham's faith was the sacrifice he was willing to make.

### 2. Abraham obeyed God at great cost! (v 6-12)

The New Testament commends Abraham for faith that was ready to obey God's Word sacrificially:

> Do you want evidence that faith without deeds is useless? Was not our ancestor Abraham considered righteous for what he did when he offered Isaac on the altar? You see that his faith and his actions were working together, and his faith was made complete by what he did. And the scripture was fulfilled that says, 'Abraham believed God, and it was credited to him as righteousness,' and he was called God's friend. **James 2 v 20-23**

Real saving faith is expressed and completed in deeds, especially when they are costly. Abraham didn't just claim to have faith or sing about his faith; he obeyed in faith, at great cost to himself and to those he loved, and so was regarded by God as His 'friend'.

It's striking that Abraham's faith was prepared to commit his wife and son to this sacrifice as well. As the heads of families, Christian men must often commit not only themselves, but also their families to making sacrifices in following Jesus. Remaining in a small urban terrace to support a faithful local church rather than following the crowd to a bigger house in the country may mean sacrifice for the whole family in terms of schools and space. Accepting a lesser-paid job for better hours to be home in time for homegroup, or giving sacrificially to finance gospel work will mean more ordinary holidays and clothes.

Asking to remove the children from certain classes at school or insisting that the kids come to church rather than play Sunday cricket may even have our wives suggesting we're becoming ugly zealots. Accepting an invitation to move to a country with a repressive regime to support the underground church could be dangerous for all the family. But sacrificial service of God is good for mums and kids as well as dads. It helps them, as well as us, to clarify their faith. God never asks more than is good for us all in becoming like Christ, and to become like Christ we have to learn sacrificial faith. And when our children are able to choose sacrificial obedience for themselves, we must not dissuade them from expressing their faith like Abraham and Jesus.

Moreover, we can't claim that our obedience is sacrificial until it hurts. This is not to look for pointless pain and sacrifice. Pain is not to be enjoyed. God forbids asceticism, the refusal to enjoy the generosity of God. Indeed it is demonic to forbid the biblical, thankful enjoyment of God's good creation (1 Timothy 4). When Jesus called His disciples, saying, 'If anyone would come after me, he must deny himself and take up his cross and follow me', He was not telling his disciples to wear hair shirts and whip themselves. Jesus was not a sadomasochist. He didn't go to the cross because He enjoyed pain. He went to the cross in obedience to God and for the salvation of others.

Likewise, in following Him, we must be prepared to suffer and make sacrifices where it is necessary in order to obey God and for the salvation of others. As with Abraham, saving faith will make costly sacrifices when it's necessary to obey God.

Dietrich Bonhoeffer, the German pastor imprisoned and finally executed for his opposition to Hitler and Nazism, wrote about this from prison in *The Cost of Discipleship*:

> Suffering then, is the badge of true discipleship. The disciple is not above his master ... that is why Luther reckoned suffering among the marks of the true church ... if we refuse to take up our cross and submit to suffering and rejection at the hands of men, we forfeit our fellowship with Christ and have ceased to follow him. But if we lose our lives in his service and carry our cross, we shall find our lives again in the fellowship of the cross with Christ. [2]

The road that Abraham travelled from Beersheba to Moriah was the way of the cross that Jesus walked and the way that every believer must follow. When God tested Abraham, He gave him the chance to purify his faith in costly obedience. That testing will come to every follower of Christ in adversity or persecution or cost. It may be the adversity of serving Christ in a difficult housing estate. It may be the persecution of a distressed family or cynical staff room. It may be the costs of weekends and evenings, money and energy, given to a youth ministry. Saving faith is always costly faith.

### 3. Abraham received from God a substitutionary sacrifice! (v 13-14)

The name of God in the passage changes at this point from *Elohim* (stressing His power) to *Jahweh* (stressing His faithfulness). Abraham was about to discover the faithfulness of God in providing a substitutionary sacrifice for Isaac on the mountain of the LORD. In the same way, the New Testament proclaims the provision of Jesus on the mountain of the LORD as our substitute. John the Baptist pointed to Jesus, proclaiming: 'Look, the Lamb of God, who takes away the sin of the world!' (John 1 v 29). Just as the faith of Abraham was provided with a substitute, so our faith in God's promise is provided with the crucified Christ who suffered the penalty for our sin.

Charles Simeon was a great 18th-19th-century preacher in Cambridge and the founder of modern expository preaching in Britain. He describes his own conversion as a young man in 1779 in terms of realising that God had provided a substitutionary lamb for him:

> What, may I transfer my guilt to another? Has God provided an offering for me, that I may lay my sins on his head? Then, God willing, I will not bear them on my own soul one moment longer. Accordingly I sought to lay my sins upon the sacred head of Jesus; and on the Wednesday began to have a hope of mercy; on the Thursday that hope increased; on the Friday and Saturday it became more strong; and on the Sunday morning, Easter-day, April 4, I awoke early with these words upon my heart and lips, 'Jesus Christ is risen today! Hallelujah! Hallelujah!' From that hour peace flowed in rich abundance into my soul; and at the Lord's table I had the sweetest access to God through my blessed saviour. [3]

I imagine that is how Abraham and Isaac felt as they descended from the hill of sacrifice. Abraham's faith was saving faith, not because his faith itself saved, but because God supplied his trust with the substitutionary sacrifice he needed.

This same sacrificial faith of Abraham is required of Christians today. Faith that God can raise the dead; faith that obeys God at great cost; faith that welcomes the death of a substitute. We must believe that God can raise us and our children from the dead. We must believe that any cost is worth paying to remain obedient to God. We must believe that God has provided a substitute for us. This is the faith of Abraham, who for his example of sacrificial faith qualifies to join 'a few good men'.

## BIBLE BACKGROUND

### *The Bible*

The holy Scriptures 'are able to make you wise for salvation through faith in Christ Jesus' (2 Timothy 3 v 15). If the whole Old Testament is the promise of Christ, the first five books by Moses clarify in particular the way of salvation through Him. The account of Abraham concentrates upon the need for faith in God's gospel promise.

### *Genesis*

Genesis presents the origins of our world and its need of a saviour in major sections. Having learnt that God is our Creator and Judge (Genesis 1-11), we learn that God made a glorious 'gospel' promise to recreate His kingdom (Genesis 12). We then learn that God is faithful to this promise (from the life of Abraham in ch 12-24), gracious to sinners (from the life of Jacob in ch 25-35), and sovereign to save (from the life of Joseph in ch 37-50). It is immediately clear that to save sinners, God has made a gospel promise that must be trusted.

### *Abraham*

The story of Abraham is dominated by the binding promise, or covenant, made to Abraham and his descendants in Genesis 12. The promise was repeated and expanded on three great occasions. In Genesis 12, God promised to bring Abraham and his descendants back into a paradise kingdom like the Garden of Eden. God promised a land, a people and blessing through which all nations would be blessed. The New Testament calls this promise of a place in God's kingdom 'the gospel' (Galatians 3). In Genesis 15 God confirmed this promise with dramatic night-time illustrations. He promised Abraham descendants as numerous as the stars in the night sky and land, guaranteed by a covenant ceremony involving a smoking pot and flaming torch. In Genesis 17 God again confirmed His promise with the ceremony of circumcision, which symbolised being cut off from sin in our hearts for faithful obedience to God.

Abraham believed this covenant promise, and God accounted to him the righteousness of Christ. So when God told Abraham to sacrifice Isaac, through whom all these promises were to be fulfilled, God was severely testing Abraham's confidence in God's promise. But Abraham maintained his confidence in God, displaying tremendous sacrificial faith in His gospel, and discovered that God is utterly faithful to raise the dead to life and respond to costly sacrifice by providing the substitute we need.

## Questions for group discussion

1. Do we believe in the resurrection of the dead?

2. Are we willing to make sacrifices for God?

3. Are we confident that Christ has suffered all the penalty for our sins as our substitute?

## References

1 Killing Fields, Living Fields, Don Cormack, Monarch Books, 1997.

2 Dietrich Bonfhoeffer, The Cost of Discipleship, SCM Press, 1990, p80.

3 Handley C. G. Moule, Charles Simeon, IVP, 1952, p25.

# 3

# SELF-DISCIPLINED JOSEPH

*'He left his cloak in her hand and ran'*

GENESIS 39 v 12

Self-discipline is perhaps not as valued as it once was. It sounds a little dull, even repressed. But even if we do tend to prize self-expression and spontaneity more than previous generations did, most of us are aware that men who make a lasting impact have usually developed great self-discipline.

The sportsman who can't control his diet and drinking won't survive in professional sport. The musician who can't discipline himself to practise will never be very good. The student who can't be self-disciplined in study will never achieve top grades. Some men go far with natural talent, but there's something very sad about those whose indiscipline means their talent never really fulfils its potential.

The same is true spiritually. Most of the men who make an impact for Jesus seem to be self-disciplined. Men like William Wilberforce (abolishing the African slave trade), Hudson Taylor (missionary to China) or John Stott (preacher and writer of countless books) have not only been gifted by God, but also marked by rugged self-discipline in their daily devotion to prayer and Bible study, moral purity and dedication to evangelism. Indeed, one suspects that their giftedness is not unrelated to their self-control. Just as a concert pianist might explain that his genius comes from practising ten hours a day, so God seems to increase the spiritual gifting of those with the self-discipline to use it.

It's no surprise, therefore, to find that self-discipline is very highly valued in Scripture. The Holy Spirit is, says Paul, 'a spirit of power, of love and of self-discipline' (2 Timothy 1 v 7). Paul tells Titus to teach both young and older men to be 'self-controlled' (Titus 2 v 2). Peter tells his readers: 'Prepare your minds for action; be self-controlled ... Be self-controlled and alert' (1 Peter 1 v 13; 5 v 8). One of the requirements repeatedly listed for church elders is that they must be 'self-controlled' (1 Timothy 3 v 2; Titus 1 v 8).

Nowhere is self-discipline more necessary for Christian men than in facing sexual temptation. One of the finest examples of such moral self-discipline is Joseph...

> Now Joseph had been taken down to Egypt. Potiphar, an Egyptian who was one of Pharaoh's officials, the captain of the guard, bought him from the Ishmaelites who had taken him there.
>
> The LORD was with Joseph and he prospered, and he lived in the house of his Egyptian master. When his master saw that the LORD was with him and that the LORD gave him success in everything he did, Joseph found favour in his eyes and became his attendant. Potiphar put him in charge of his household, and he entrusted to his care everything he owned. From the time he put him in charge of his household and of all that he owned, the LORD blessed the household of the Egyptian because of Joseph. The blessing of the LORD was on everything Potiphar had, both in the house and in the field. So he left in Joseph's care everything he had; with Joseph in charge, he did not concern himself with anything except the food he ate.
>
> Now Joseph was well-built and handsome, and after a while his master's wife took notice of Joseph and said, 'Come to bed with me!'
>
> But he refused. 'With me in charge,' he told her, 'my master does not concern himself with anything in the house; everything he owns he has entrusted to my care. No one is greater in this house than I am. My master has withheld nothing from me except you, because you are his wife. How then could I do such a wicked thing and sin against God?' And though she spoke to Joseph day after day, he refused to go to bed with her or even to be with her.

One day he went into the house to attend to his duties, and none of the household servants was inside. She caught him by his cloak and said, 'Come to bed with me!' But he left his cloak in her hand and ran out of the house.

When she saw that he had left his cloak in her hand and had run out of the house, she called her household servants. 'Look,' she said to them, 'this Hebrew has been brought to us to make sport of us! He came in here to sleep with me, but I screamed. When he heard me scream for help, he left his cloak beside me and ran out of the house.'

She kept his cloak beside her until his master came home. Then she told him this story: 'That Hebrew slave you brought us came to me to make sport of me. But as soon as I screamed for help, he left his cloak beside me and ran out of the house.'

When his master heard the story his wife told him, saying, 'This is how your slave treated me,' he burned with anger. Joseph's master took him and put him in prison, the place where the king's prisoners were confined.

But while Joseph was there in the prison, the LORD was with him; he showed him kindness and granted him favour in the eyes of the prison warder. So the warder put Joseph in charge of all those held in the prison, and he was made responsible for all that was done there. The warder paid no attention to anything under Joseph's care, because the LORD was with Joseph and gave him success in whatever he did. **Genesis 39 v 1-23**

*As the prisoners laboured in the prison workshop, their Hebrew overseer could see with satisfaction that his new Creative Programme was well received. Joseph was virtually in charge now, and guards and prisoners alike deferred to him, even though he returned to his cell each night. Joseph knew that once more his surprising promotion, even within this Egyptian jail, was down to the presence of the LORD.*

*While the other prisoners were absorbed in their weaving and carving projects, Joseph reflected upon his crazy up-and-down* life. He recalled his childhood in Canaan with his many brothers. His parents, Jacob and Rachel, had doted on him. His father had foolishly made Joseph his favourite, even giving him a special gorgeous multi-coloured coat to parade around in. Joseph had been so spoilt he didn't notice how he was irritating his brothers.

As a teenager he had often got his brothers into trouble with their father and then infuriated everyone with his weird dreams about his own family bowing down to him in the future. On reflection, it was hardly surprising that they'd finally got rid of him. Near Dothan they threw him down a well and then sold him to Ishmaelite traders. They'd been planning to kill him, but Reuben had tried to defend him, and then Judah, very much the leader, had persuaded them all to sell him. Joseph wondered what story they could possibly have told his poor father.

But life in Egypt had turned out rather well. Potiphar had proved to be a great master. The LORD must have been behind Joseph's meteoric rise, for he was soon appointed chief steward over the whole household! Potiphar was a decorated soldier, captain of Pharaoh's elite Royal Guard, and his massive home overlooking the Nile was palatial. Joseph's gift for administration was proving immensely helpful and Potiphar favoured him hugely. Joseph had his own comfortable rooms and enjoyed the total confidence of Potiphar. If only his brothers could see him, dressed in Egyptian silk, bossing the maids and gardeners and cooks around as if he owned the place.

But then there was Mrs Potiphar. He'd worried about her from the moment he arrived. She was quite an attractive woman, younger than her husband and with nothing better to do than lunch with her friends and gossip about clothes and houses and affairs. It wasn't long before he could feel her eying him up.

She began flirting outrageously with him and it became more and more uncomfortable, for she was quite seductive. He was a normal guy. He felt as sexually frustrated as any single man. He often cried out to the LORD at night to somehow find him a wife, but he knew that few slaves were ever allowed to marry. In fact, Egyptian culture seemed to smile on wealthy owners using their slaves like a harem if they wanted.

Sometimes he fantasised about being with her. No one back home would ever know. He wondered if the LORD had forgotten him, anyway. He'd had a rough time and occasionally felt sorry for himself. If he kept refusing Mrs P he could get in a lot of trouble. And sometimes when she walked around the house, she was wearing almost nothing. Joseph's eyes would be popping and his heart racing as he tried not to look. But she dressed like that deliberately – usually when Potiphar had gone to work.

But as Joseph lay in bed at night, he worked out a few simple things. Potiphar had been good to him and she was his wife. He couldn't betray the captain's trust. Sleeping with her could only end in trouble with Potiphar and she'd be sure to dump him in a moment.

And it was wrong – wicked, in fact. The LORD had been kind to Joseph and he couldn't now betray God with adultery. He had to calmly clarify his thoughts when she wasn't flaunting herself in front of him, and plan his strategy. He would have to avoid her as much as possible, and if she tried anything, just leg it. It was best just to run – she was too attractive and persuasive for him to try to talk her out of it. He knew he was too vulnerable. He daily prayed for strength to hold to his convictions and to carry out his planned responses.

One day, she just blatantly asked him for sex. "Come to bed with me," she said in that honey-coated voice of hers. There was no shame in her at all. Thankfully, Joseph had rehearsed his lines and he explained why he couldn't. He owed too much to Potiphar and to the LORD. "How then could I do such a wicked thing and sin against God?' he said, and managed to escape as two of the maids walked in to make the beds.

After that, he kept as much out of her way as possible, trying only to be near her when others were around. But he could sense *that his refusal had only inflamed her desire. One day, he had to check the bedlinen in the master's rooms and she was there, waiting for him alone. Wearing nothing but a flimsy silk robe, she just threw herself at him and started kissing him. He managed to disentangle himself and ran out of the house. But in the process, she grabbed his robe and he had to leave it with her. He guessed that this could be incriminating. What was it with coats and him? And as he fled the house, he knew that she'd gone too far to let it rest now.*

*The captain summoned him later that night in a furious rage. It appeared that his wife claimed that he had attempted to rape her, and all the servants were backing her story. Joseph knew that slaves were usually executed for such a crime. When Potiphar condemned him to the royal prison, though, he sensed not only that Potiphar was being merciful towards his finest slave, but also that he was not wholly convinced by his wife's version of events.*

*As Joseph went over and over his actions, he was convinced he'd done the right thing. That woman was always going to be trouble and by doing the right thing, he'd probably got away in better shape than he ever would by sleeping with her. But, most importantly, his conscience was clear and his relationship with the LORD was better than ever.*

*God knew what He was doing. The LORD would look after him and could give him a wife when the time was right. God knew how lonely and frustrated he felt. He must have His reasons for wanting him single for now. If he'd rebelled against the LORD he'd now have nowhere to turn. And that great promise of a place in the kingdom of God made to his father, and his grandfather Isaac, and great-grandfather Abraham before him, would never include him if he abandoned the LORD.*

*And so he'd escaped the sword and ended up here. From exaltation to humiliation. He wondered where the LORD would take him next? And now he was running Pharaoh's prison and meeting all kinds of interesting government officials who were current-*

*ly out of favour. He was learning loads about how the Egyptian empire operated. It certainly seemed strange to be running a state prison so soon after running a military household. It was as if he was being trained for something!*

---

*Joseph and the Amazing Technicolor Dreamcoat* is a fantastically popular musical by Tim Rice and Andrew Lloyd Webber. Who can forget those memorable songs about *'Jacob, Jacob and sons, a remarkable family in anyone's book'*! The temptation of Joseph by Potiphar's wife (played by Joan Collins in the Donny Osmond classic video release) in an exotic Egyptian villa particularly lends itself to the musical format.

But the biblical record of Joseph's historic rise to the position of prime minister of Egypt, in time to help God's chosen family during a severe famine, serves another purpose. Joseph's exaltation demonstrates God's sovereign control of all circumstances so as to provide the saviour that His people would need. From a 17-year-old spoiled braggart to revered ruler of superpower Egypt, Joseph learnt that God is in control.

God worked through dreams revealing the future, through the hatred of his brothers, the lust of Potiphar's wife, the failures of the royal cupbearer, the weather that brought famine, the sleep patterns of Pharaoh and the political structures of Egypt, all to have his chosen but despised saviour exalted to power. As Joseph said to his astonished brothers when they came to Egypt:

> Do not be distressed and do not be angry with yourselves for selling me here, because it was to save lives that God sent me ahead of you. For two years now there has been famine in the land, and for the next five years there will not be ploughing and reaping. But God sent me ahead of you to preserve for you a remnant on earth and to save your lives by a great deliverance. **Genesis 45 v 5-7**

This plan of salvation would be repeated in the experience of God's Son, our own Saviour and Lord.

## The LORD was with Joseph (v 2-3, 21, 23)

Four times in this chapter we are told that the LORD was with Joseph. We are told it twice at the beginning, when he is honoured and successful in Potiphar's house, and twice at the end, when he is honoured and successful in Pharaoh's prison. Joseph had to learn that, wherever he was, through ups and downs, God was always with him. We too must learn that in promotion or sacking, profit or loss, birth or bereavement, joy or sadness, success or disappointment, God is always with us, too. Because of this, nothing is really accidental. Nothing is actually fate. Whether or not we ever understand what God is doing, He has His purposes in everything that happens to us, for 'in all things God works for the good of those who love him, who have been called according to his purpose ... to be conformed to the likeness of his Son' (Romans 8 v 28-29).

Indeed, in Joseph's life, there was a repeated pattern of exaltation followed by humiliation and then exaltation, just as there would be in the life of our Saviour, Jesus. From favourite son of Jacob (exaltation), Joseph was sold to Midianite traders as a slave (humiliation), then put in charge of Potiphar's house (exaltation), then thrown into prison for supposed assault (humiliation), from where he would be put in charge of the prison (exaltation), but then forgotten as a slave in the prison (humiliation), then finally exalted to be ruler over all Egypt (exaltation).

This would also be the pattern for the people of Israel: exalted under Joseph, humiliated in later slavery, but then exalted again under Moses. But supremely this pattern would be fulfilled in the Son of God: exalted in glory before becoming a man to be humiliated on the cross, but then rising to be exalted to rule over all with the name above all names (Philippians 2 v 5-11). It is God's way to exalt His humbled but faithful servants.

But critical to Joseph's qualification to be Israel's saviour is his early resistance to the temptations of Potiphar's wife in chapter 39, just as Jesus had to resist the temptations of Satan at the beginning of His saving ministry (Matthew 4). Joseph had to learn self-discipline and self-control in Potiphar's house if he was ever to be ruler in Pharaoh's house. He had to learn self-discipline in smaller responsibilities if he was ever to be entrusted with greater responsibilities. He had to learn how to govern himself before he would be ready to govern the world.

## The LORD gave Joseph success in everything (v 1-6)

The scene is set in 39 v 1-6 with three repeated words: 'LORD', 'Joseph' and 'everything'. The LORD was in control throughout; Joseph was the constant focus of God's attention and care; and everything was entrusted to Joseph, for nothing is beyond God's gift. That is why he and we can be content in all circumstances.

The future of Joseph and the salvation of Israel would now depend on how Joseph resisted the temptations of Potiphar's wife, just as the salvation of all Christians was dependent upon the resistance of Jesus to Satan's temptation to avoid the cross.

### *Joseph was under familiar pressures*

Let's recognise that Joseph was under many familiar pressures to give in to sin. Here was a Hebrew Brad Pitt, a young, fit, handsome man, who could have really enjoyed the adoration of this woman. He presumably had sexual needs with little prospect of ever marrying. He was far from home and no one was ever likely to find out what he did. He was far from any believers in the LORD and, having been sold into slavery, he could feel that God had abandoned him, that he'd been badly treated and was now entitled to a little pleasure.

And everyone else was doing it – sexual favours were normally expected of Egyptian slaves. There was no shame or guilt attached to it. Moreover, it could be dangerous to refuse. The wife of the captain of Pharaoh's guard was a powerful woman. It would not be wise to upset or offend her. And her sustained seductions and eventual passionate attack upon him would have been reasonable excuses to surrender to her offers of pleasure. No doubt she was very seductive, and sex with her would be very exciting. These were familiar pressures upon Joseph to surrender to sin. Perhaps, by comparison, we have fewer excuses than we thought. The invitation to sex in verse 7 is crude and blunt, but Joseph still persisted.

### Joseph said, "No!"

Joseph resisted her seduction with simple self-discipline: 'he refused'. In the end, self-discipline is the ability to say 'No!'

The explosive England rugby union and former Wigan rugby league star Jason Robinson is a committed Christian. In his autobiography, *Finding my Feet*, he describes the difference made by Christ to his life. Before he became a Christian, he was wild and dissolute, 'morally bankrupt' and 'shallow', as he puts it. But after finding forgiveness in Jesus, largely through the quiet witness of his Wigan teammate 'Inga' Tuigamala, this all changed. He remarks with great insight:

> People often think that because of my devotion to Christianity, my life must be restricted, but I feel freer now than I have ever done. I can say yes or no – I couldn't say no before.[1]

Like Jason, by the strength of God, Joseph found he was able to say 'No' as well. We learn from the text how he did this.

He resisted temptation because he had prepared two convictions for his heart and two responses for his body. These convictions and responses are hugely helpful for us today.

### Joseph had prepared his convictions to refuse temptation!

There were two convictions behind Joseph's self-discipline which gave him strength to resist. He had clearly thought about them already and was able to state them. We can't expect to resist temptation if we refuse to prepare our defence. Indeed, most battles with immorality are lost long before the actual opportunity for sin presents itself. For example, if we are getting ready to go out to a bar or club and already thinking about what it would be like if we got undressed, then, if the opportunity arrives, we've already lost.

If I'm at work thinking about the porn I could watch later on, I shouldn't be surprised that I can't resist when I get home and sit in front of the TV, surfing channels with my remote. If I haven't discussed any guidelines with my girlfriend about not being alone together in her room, then I won't be able to resist my desires (or hers) when we're in the flat late Saturday night and her flatmates are away for the weekend.

We need to prepare our defensive convictions long before the temptation strikes. We need to organise our resistance when we are not under pressure, when we are feeling spiritually stronger in the light of day. We could ask Christian mates or church leaders what they would do. Many men would avoid crashing into immorality if they rang their wives from the office to discuss where they're going after work or asked them to block the dodgy TV channels (less embarrassing, too) or called their girlfriends to discuss the guidelines during the day and not at one o'clock in the morning after intimate prayer and two glasses of wine!

As the management consultants might say: 'Fail to prepare and prepare to fail' (and then charge you a million pounds for saying it!). Joseph had planned his response. Perhaps he had struggled to come to his convictions, but when the temptress struck, his defences were ready.

### 1. He had considered his debt to Potiphar (v 8-9)

Joseph was well aware of the privileges he enjoyed under Potiphar, which would be lost if he abused his master's kindness: 'everything he owns he has entrusted to my care.' It is only sensible to consider the damage that will follow from sexual misbehaviour. The idea that an affair might spice up a marriage is pernicious nonsense.

All the couples affected by adultery whom I have met have been absolutely devastated by it. Most had never realised what carnage it would bring to all their relationships and especially to any children involved.

The damage is only slightly smaller for single people. The wreckage caused by an affair at work can ruin a promising career. The guilt and misery in a Christian can be catastrophic. And then there is sometimes a sexually-transmitted disease or pregnancy to face. Don't believe the glossy lies of those who have no alternative but to justify themselves. There is nothing glamorous about an affair. Just considering the likely pain and damage is enough to help us avoid it like the plague.

Joseph also recognised the sustained benefits of honouring his master. He would not surrender these long-term benefits for some short-term illicit pleasure. This is wisdom. So often, men ruin their whole lives for an orgasm! I know Christian men who have wrecked their marriage because of a stupid affair at work that never lasted; another got a girl pregnant and she had an abortion, all because of a crazy late-night binge; others have lost their opportunity of church office or training in ministry because of a deeply-regretted temporary relationship. And nearly every failure is fuelled by drink. Alcohol reduces our inhibitions. In moderation this may help the intimacy of a marriage (*Song of Songs* celebrates it), but it's crazy for anyone wanting to resist temptation. Instead of such short-sightedness, Joseph had stopped to appreciate the long-term benefits of remaining faithful to Potiphar.

Joseph also considered his obligation to Potiphar: 'My master has withheld nothing from me except you, because you are his wife.' He recognised the ingratitude of abusing the trust shown in him by his master. Having been treated so kindly, it would be wretchedly dishonourable to take advantage of the man's kindness and sleep with his wife. It is worth remembering who else will be wronged by our immorality. Behind the married woman flirting with us at a work social is a husband and children. She may be too drunk to remember them, but their lives will be shattered by the divorce. After your girlfriend has split up with you, she will want to marry another man, perhaps a lovely Christian. He will be so disappointed that you have already slept with his wife-to-be. And she will be bitterly disappointed on her wedding day, even if it is you she is standing next to. We won't want the baggage of comparative images in our heads when we make love to our wives and neither will those we sin with. We need to show some respect to those who will be hurt by our stupid lack of self-discipline.

Joseph recognised that Potiphar would be wronged and it helped him refuse the temptation. If only Christian men facing temptation today could think beyond the next few hours of pleasure (apparently it's ruined by the guilt anyway) and beyond themselves to those who will suffer. Joseph had considered his debt to Potiphar.

### 2. He had considered his debt to God (v 9)
Joseph followed his description of his privileged life with a refusal to sin against God. He knew that his lifestyle was a blessing from God, and that he could not expect that blessing to continue if he rebelled against God. Neither can we.

He recognised and named the true nature of what Potiphar's wife was proposing. This wasn't 'a bit of fun', 'just playing around', 'being adult', or whatever other euphemism we might hear. It wasn't even 'going to bed'; it was 'a wicked thing'. Joseph said, 'You are his wife. How then could I do such a wicked thing and sin against God?'

Sexual pleasure is for marriage. God designed sex as a wonderful kind of physical and emotional glue to stick a husband and wife together. When married men are not getting enough at home, we need to work at our marriage relationship, not start wishing we were with someone else. It's not her fault. It's ours. Outside the lifelong partnership of a man and a woman, sex is wickedly wrong and an offence against God that deserves His punishment. Even if for Christians that penalty has been suffered by Christ, we can expect our loving heavenly Father to severely discipline His sons who misbehave 'because the Lord disciplines those he loves' (Hebrews 12 v 6). And we may well be fooling ourselves when we think we are Christians. Paul wrote:

> Do not be deceived: Neither the sexually immoral nor idolaters nor adulterers, nor male prostitutes nor homosexual offenders nor thieves nor the greedy nor drunkards nor slanderers nor swindlers will inherit the kingdom of God. And that is what some of you were.
> **1 Corinthians 6 v 9-10**

A Christian may have had a sexually immoral lifestyle in the past. But if it continues unrepented, he is not a Christian. Thankfully, for the repentant there is total pardon.

Joseph displayed an appreciation of debts to both Potiphar and God. The apostle Paul explains that the kindness and grace of God in Christ is likewise what motivates Christians to say 'No!' to immorality:

> For the grace of God that brings salvation has appeared to all men. It teaches us to say 'No' to ungodliness and worldly passions, and to live self-controlled, upright and godly lives in this present age, while we wait for the blessed hope – the glorious appearing of our great God and Saviour, Jesus Christ, who gave himself for us to redeem us from all wickedness and to purify for himself a people that are his very own, eager to do what is good. **Titus 2 v 11-14**

Since God has been so kind and gracious to us, even if many of the benefits are future, we need to respond by being the kind of people Christ wants us to be. He actually died to redeem a people who want to do good. He doesn't want us to remain in the immorality that is common to pagan unbelievers. His grace and kindness motivate us to say 'No!' as Joseph did.

If we prepare our convictions about our debts, both to those who will be damaged by our sin and to God, who has been so kind and generous to us, we will refuse temptation like Joseph.

**Joseph had prepared his responses to avoid temptation!**

It's not clever to overestimate our capacity to resist sin. This is particularly the case with sexual temptation, because God has designed us to find women attractive and to enjoy sex within marriage. When the society we live in isn't playing by God's rules, we are often much more vulnerable than we think. Joseph very wisely attempted to avoid temptation not only with prepared theological convictions, but also with prepared physical responses.

### *1. He avoided the temptress (v 10)*

'And though she spoke to Joseph day after day, he refused to go to bed with her or even to be with her.' The temptation was incessant, so Joseph avoided her. We can't expect to hold out forever. Joseph didn't think he could persuade her to think differently. So he avoided her. Likewise, we must avoid the sources of temptation, which will be different for each of us.

For some, it will mean avoiding the shop where the temptation to buy pornographic magazines or DVDs is too strong. For others, it will mean not buying a computer without having a 'Net Nanny' installed with an accountability programme that reports usage to a trusted friend. I have an evangelist friend who, when staying in hotels abroad, asks at reception for the TV to be removed from his room before he goes in to ensure he can't watch what he shouldn't. The same practice might be a good idea at home! Christian friends can be helpful in asking one another about work relationships or blocked porn channels (and wives need to realise how many normal men struggle).

Too many men operate on the edge of trouble, seeing how close they can get. But playing with sin is as stupid as playing with a deadly snake poised to strike. We might get away with it a few times, but eventually we'll get bitten. That's what snakes do, and it's what sin does, too. Too often we think it's deliciously dangerous to be in places or with people who are bound to get us into trouble eventually. We should never have gone there with her, or with them. And we should have gone home long ago.

The story is told of an Australian billionaire with a luxury yacht based in Sydney Harbour who was interviewing potential helmsmen for his yacht. As the best three applicants gathered on the boat to demonstrate their sailing skills to him, he explained that he wanted a sailor of great ability who would be available to take him and his friends or clients out sailing whenever he was home in Sydney. The successful applicant would, of course, be rewarded handsomely.

Each of the three men took turns to showcase his skills. The first sailed the priceless yacht at top speed within 100 metres of the rocky cliffs and everyone gasped at his amazing talent. When the second helmsman took over, he sailed the yacht within 50 metres of the cliffs and everyone was breathless with excitement. What could the third applicant do? Calmly the third man steered the luxury boat out into the middle of the harbour and they all enjoyed a rather relaxing trip across the bay, admiring the view.

At the end of the trials, the hopefuls gathered to hear the billionaire's verdict. To their great surprise, he gave the third applicant the job. He explained his decision: 'You were all amazingly skillful. But my yacht is precious to me and I don't want a helmsman who is so confident that he is tempted to steer it within a few metres of crashing on the rocks. One mistake and it's a disaster. I want a man who will take it out into the open water and enjoy the safety and beauty that is there!'

In the same way, God doesn't want us to be driving our precious bodies as close to immorality as we think is possible. We may get away with it for a while, but one mistake and we live with that disaster forever. Actually, there is great joy and satisfaction in living well within God's rules and keeping sex for marriage. So why are you seeing that colleague after work for a drink when you know she'll flirt with you and you fancy her? Why are you sharing a flat with girls? Why did you appoint that attractive secretary? Why are you going on holiday with your fiancée? (Don't tell me you'll stay in separate sleeping-bags!) Why have you agreed to go clubbing with colleagues while you're abroad on business when you know you'll feel pressured to drink too much and go to a strip joint? Why haven't you asked your wife to block the TV channels and your Bible-study leader to get your XXX porn watch reports? Why are you sharing your personal thoughts with some-one else's wife, and why are you stopping to chat when you drop her off after church? Stop steering so close to the rocks. You're in grave danger of crashing your life and the lives of others on the rocks of immorality.

### 2. He fled from the temptress (v 12)

If avoidance was Joseph's first strategic response, running away was his fall-back alternative. 'She caught him by his cloak and said, "Come to bed with me!" But he left his cloak in her hand and ran out of the house.' Sometimes the best option is to run. No discussion, no negotiation, no experimentation – just get away fast. Paul told the Corinthians: 'Flee from sexual immorality' and 'Flee from idolatry', and Timothy, 'Flee the evil desires of youth' (probably primarily argumentativeness but including immorali-ty). As a wise army commander knows that it's best to leave the field of battle when faced with insurmountable odds, so the wise man knows when he is better off getting away.

I heard recently of a young husband who realised that while being away from his wife he was tempted to sin, so he drove 200 miles home late at night to be in bed with her. She was shocked, but he had done exactly the right thing. I recall quickly having to leave a lawyers' social dinner in the City of London when strip-pers arrived. What struck me afterwards was that some of the other men admitted that they wished they'd fled with me, for they were now wracked with guilt for staying. The best thing that Joseph did that day was to run. We're not told whether he was running only to avoid the woman's advances or also to avoid his own weakening resolve. But there's nothing admirable about thinking we can resist sexual immorality. We need to learn from Joseph to run from particular situations, people, shops and computers if we suspect that we may fall into sexual immorality.

The secret of Joseph's self-discipline was prepared convictions and responses. He considered his obligation to the people involved and to God. And he planned how to avoid temptation or flee from it. If we follow that pattern ourselves, we will be able to resist sexual temptation as Joseph did.

Of course, as a result of Mrs Potiphar's false testimony, Joseph was thrown into prison. It can sometimes be costly being godly, because we make enemies of those who want to sin. But when Joseph got to prison, he discovered that the LORD was waiting for him. And the same pattern of blessing and preparation for office continued. Joseph was put in charge and was so successful that the prison warder entrusted everyone and everything to him. The point is that, even if we suffer from the ungodly for resistance to sin, we shall be blessed by the LORD, in this life or the next. And eventually this self-disciplined Hebrew was made prime minister of Egypt and, more importantly, saviour of God's people. The man who was rejected by his brothers, the servant who was raised to be ruler, was, as Joseph explained to his brothers, part of God's sovereign plan: 'You intended to harm me, but God intended it for good to accomplish what is now being done, the saving of many lives' (50 v 20). Joseph had to learn self-discipline for this role, and so did the Saviour to come.

Men who are useful to God and His people will be sexually controlled, self-disciplined men like Joseph. For his sexual self-discipline in a sexually immoral context, Joseph belongs among 'a few good men'.

# BIBLE BACKGROUND

## *The Bible*

The Scriptures are 'able to make [us] wise for salvation' (2 Timothy 3 v 15), principally by showing us the Saviour. For, as Jesus said of the Old Testament:'These are the Scriptures that testify about me' (John 5 v 39). The risen Jesus turned to the same Scriptures to explain His death and resurrection: 'Everything must be fulfilled that is written about me in the Law of Moses, the Prophets and the Psalms' (Luke 24 v 44, referring to the Hebrew divisions of the Old Testament). The account of Joseph helps us to understand not just the man who was elevated to the position of prime minister of Egypt, but also the man who is now Lord of the universe: Jesus.

## *Genesis*

The God revealed in Genesis is our Creator who must punish sin (Genesis 1-11). But He is also the God of Abraham, faithful to His gospel promise (ch 12-22); the God of Jacob, gracious to sinners (ch 25-35); and the God of Joseph, sovereign to save (ch 37-50). The story of Joseph demonstrates that through injustice, humiliation and exaltation, in dreams, family relationships, weather systems and the political structures of superpowers, all that happens to him is 'according to the plan of him who works out everything in conformity with the purpose of his will' (Ephesians 1 v 11).

## *Joseph*

Joseph is the despised servant who is exalted to be the saviour of God's people. The three stages of Joseph's exaltation in Egypt were each recognised with an acknowledgment of his power by the rest of his family (just as Jesus' family of Christians is expected to acknowledge Him): in Genesis 42 v 1-38, ten brothers bow before him; in 43 v 1 – 45 v 28, eleven brothers bow before him; in 46 v 1-27, the whole family bows before him – just as his boyhood dreams had foretold. Joseph described the wickedness of his brothers in these terms: 'You intended to harm me, but God intended it for good to accomplish what is now being done, the saving of many lives' (Genesis 50 v 20). These words foretell the future Saviour, betrayed by His brothers to death on a cross, so accomplishing the LORD's sovereign plan of salvation. Joseph teaches us about Jesus. And just as Joseph had to resist temptation to seek pleasure for himself, Jesus had to do the same throughout His life.

## Questions for group discussion

**1.** How are people hurt by sexual immorality?

**2.** How does God's grace motivate us to sexual self-discipline?

**3.** How can we avoid sexual temptation?

**4.** When do we need to run away from temptation?

### *References*

1 Jason Robinson, *Finding My Feet*, Coronet Books, 2003, p71, 239.

# 4 UNWORLDLY MOSES

*'He persevered because he saw him who is invisible'*

HEBREWS 11 v 27

We might think that being called a man of the world is a compliment. Our culture respects 'a man of the world' as someone who is mature and wise, someone who understands the grim realities of life, who understands women and how to attract them, who understands money and how to get it.

But God's view of a 'man of the world' is very different:

> You adulterous people, don't you know that friendship with the world is hatred towards God? Anyone who chooses to be a friend of the world becomes an enemy of God! **James 4 v 4**

The world and God are alternatives. We cannot love both. We must love one or the other. If we're devoted to this world, we're not devoted to God! We need to know why.

In Scripture, the world is seen as created by God to reflect His glory. It still belongs to God and is governed and blessed by Him. But led by sinful mankind, the world is now in disordered rebellion against God and is currently enslaved by evil spiritual forces promoting ideas opposed to God.

At the heart of worldly thinking is the enthronement of material things – people, pleasure and property – as the objects of our worship in the place of God. So people of the world pursue ideal partners, ideal holidays and ideal houses. These things are not wrong in themselves, for they are the gifts of God. But the nature of sin is to displace our Creator with created things, which is idolatry. Mankind is in bondage to this idolatry until we are liberated by the teachings of Christ.

Such worldly idolatry exalts human ideas about creation (in materialism), about truth (in secularism), and about God (in pluralism):

- **materialism** is the belief that material things are all that exist or matter, seen in the popularity of Richard Dawkins' *The God Delusion*. It leads to hedonism, which is the pursuit of sensual pleasures, eg: the rise of 'lads' mags' which reflect a passion for sex, cars and sport. Hedonism encourages covetousness that lusts for more. Porn and shopping will thrive in this world.

- **secularism** is the view that spiritual issues are matters of personal opinion or institutional conspiracy that cannot be verified, seen in the popularity of Dan Brown's *The Da Vinci Code*. It leads to privatism, which is the refusal to allow faith in God to be openly preached or debated (spiritual censorship), eg: television chat shows will endlessly debate all manner of moral, political and social issues without any reference to the existence and authority of God. Privatism encourages ignorance that won't consider serious spiritual and eternal issues. Brutishness and prejudice will thrive in this world.

- **pluralism** is the view that all religions are equally valid ways to God, seen in Booker Prize-winner Yann Martel's *Life of Pi*. It leads to ritualism, which is a respect for the pathetic ceremonial practices of countless empty religions, eg: the teaching of comparative religion in schools by comparing the ceremonial roles of holy books, places and leaders of each religion, rather than actually considering spiritual beliefs. This encourages pride, which assumes that we are all spiritually secure in whatever we believe. Aggressive minority beliefs (eg: Islam) and practices (eg: homosexuality) will thrive in this world.

The effect of worldliness in our heads is materialism, secularism and pluralism. But the effect of this worldliness on our hearts is covetousness, ignorance and pride. We see this worldliness absolutely everywhere in our nation! But God is not impressed: 'For the wisdom of this world is foolishness in God's sight' (1 Corinthians 3 v 19).

However, God still loved this world so much as to send His Son to die for His people in it. He defeated the prince of this world on the cross. He empowers His people to go into this world as His salt and light, to be in the world for Christ, but not of it. We are to overcome the lies of this world and seek the world to come, the kingdom of God in the new creation. This presents every man with a choice: to live for God or for this world. We cannot do both. Jesus thought the choice was obvious: 'What good will it be for a man if he gains the whole world, yet forfeits his soul?' (Matthew 16 v 26).

Now many Christians protest at this choice. Surely God loved this world enough to send His Son. Surely the world to come is this creation renewed, redeemed and resurrected. This is true. But God does not love this world and its people as they are. He will destroy this world before renewing it and will send its unrepentant citizens to hell. God's love is committed to changing the world and its people. So we must love the world, its cities and its peoples enough to want them transformed. But if we love the world and its ideology as it is, then we are not loving God. I am aware that theologians have debated various models of Christian relationship with the world:

- **Christ opposed to the world** – with Christians being counter-cultural. I think we *do* want Christian media, arts and colleges to commend God's ways.
- **Christ in the world** – with Christians celebrating His presence in culture. I think we should recognise God's 'common grace' in enabling secular justice, etc.
- **Christ above the world** – with Christians supplementing culture. I think we do want Christians to introduce legislation driven by Christian principles.

- **Christ in parallel with the world** – with Christians preaching to the culture. I think we also want to proclaim the biblical truth modelled in church life.
- **Christ transforming culture** – with Christians working within the culture. I think we should want to be involved in shaping the philosophy of our laws and culture.

Surely all these approaches have some support in Scripture, though each has real dangers as well. We must be careful to ensure that, like God, we love the world, its cities and its people sufficiently to want them to be transformed in Christ. We must not love this world and its idolatrous ideology as it is. For the apostle John is very clear:

> Do not love the world or anything in the world. If anyone loves the world, the love of the Father is not in him. For everything in the world – the cravings of sinful man, the lust of his eyes and the boasting of what he has and does – comes not from the Father but from the world. The world and its desires pass away, but the man who does the will of God lives for ever. **1 John 2 v 15-17**

Perhaps the clearest example of a man in the Bible rejecting this world and its idolatrous ideology is Moses. This particular aspect of his life is most fully addressed in Hebrews 11, where the writer reflects upon the description of Moses in Exodus. His attitudes and decisions are of immense value to Christian men living in our prosperous Western culture today.

> By faith Moses, when he had grown up, refused to be known as the son of Pharaoh's daughter. He chose to be ill-treated along with the people of God rather than to enjoy the pleasures of sin for a short time. He regarded disgrace for the sake of Christ as of greater value than the treasures of Egypt, because he was looking ahead to his reward. By faith he left Egypt, not fearing the king's anger; he persevered because he saw him who is invisible. By faith he kept the Passover and the sprinkling of blood, so that the destroyer of the firstborn would not touch the firstborn of Israel. **Hebrews 11 v 24-28**

*All around Moses' rickety cart, the slow mass exodus of a slave people continued. Hundreds of thousands of people of all ages, emaciated and poorly dressed but with bright hope in their eyes, were walking out of Egypt. They were free at last. Some were on newly-acquired thoroughbred horses. Most were on mules or on foot, walking beside carts piled high with unfamiliar gifts from Egyptians desperate to see the back of them.*

*As Moses steered his own mule carefully to avoid the hordes of children running excitedly among the long procession of animals and vehicles, he felt overwhelmed by the joy of leading this dishevelled refugee Hebrew people. From every direction, people offered thanks and honoured him with little gifts. They knew that through him, the LORD had liberated them from four centuries of humiliating slavery. A new life with God was before them, and they owed their deliverance in great measure to this former prince of Egypt.*

*As Moses sat with his wife Zipporah, holding the latest of their grandchildren in her arms, he contemplated the extraordinary changes brought to his life by the LORD. He had enjoyed such immense privileges as a child in the palatial home of Pharaoh's daughter. He'd received the finest education that money could buy and every comfort available in the royal household (even though he had discovered early on that he was an abandoned Hebrew baby adopted by Pharaoh's daughter during the great slaughter of Hebrew infants by her neurotic father). He'd ridden the finest horses and fastest chariots in the country. He'd learnt the political strategies and religious philosophies of the Egyptian Empire. He was being groomed for high office and perhaps even the throne. But the LORD God of Israel had also nurtured in him a growing awareness that his wealth and luxury were provided only on the scarred and bony backs of the Hebrew slaves, his own people.*

And when he'd read the accounts of Abraham, Isaac and Jacob, whose family had come to Egypt in the days of the legendary Hebrew premier, Joseph, Moses was awakened to the existence of the LORD God Almighty. He'd become so troubled by the brutally harsh treatment of his own people that he'd begun to visit their compounds in Goshen. He hoped to relieve their plight. Eventually, he was overwhelmed with the sense that the LORD's promises to their patriarchs would surely be fulfilled. He belonged with these slaves – not with their masters.

And so, on that fateful day when he fought and killed that vicious foreman, he had to choose. He chose the slaves. He'd left for Midian where he'd met his beloved Zipporah. There his royal background counted for nothing. Her father, Jethro, rather enjoyed having this sophisticated Egyptian among them. He was useless on the farm but he brought some social graces that they'd all enjoyed.

But he was no longer a prince, but plain Moses. No longer any servants or concubines to attend to his needs. Rough clothes and long hours of hard work just staying alive were now his daily routine. But the hope of living in the kingdom of God had become his ambition and reinforced his decision. He knew that Pharaoh would kill him if he could find him. He certainly missed family and friends. But the pleasures and treasures of Egypt were empty; they promised much but delivered little, and Moses longed to know God.

And then, after 40 years in Midian, the LORD had revealed himself to Moses in that burning bush and the rest was now legend – the confrontations with the new Pharaoh and the months of increasingly terrifying plagues. But Pharaoh's heart became harder and harder to the LORD, while Moses' heart was softened to His patience.

Finally, the catastrophic events of last night. As the LORD had promised, he had visited Egypt in devastating judgment, killing all the firstborn sons there. Since Pharaoh would not let the LORD's *firstborn, Israel, go free, the LORD would now strike down Pharaoh's firstborn to finally force his hand. Thankfully, God had provided the means of survival for Israel in the blood of the lambs painted on their homes. There were a lot of boys sitting rather quietly with their relieved parents in the carts around him.*

*And as Moses looked around at this horde of refugees, his heart went out to them. They were nowhere near as impressive, and certainly not as wealthy, as the Egyptians. But this was a people of faith in the LORD's promises, their future entirely in the hands of God. Moses knew he was despised and now hated amongst his old Egyptian friends. But Moses would rather travel in shame and poverty with these people on their way to meet and worship the LORD than acquire all the treasures of the Egyptian empire. He knew it seemed odd. But he was no longer living for this world, but for another: a heavenly country and a Redeemer yet to come.*

---

The brilliant 1998 DreamWorks animation *The Prince of Egypt* captures well the privileged and luxurious sort of life that Moses must have enjoyed in the home of Pharaoh's daughter where he grew up. But he walked away from the finest that this world has to offer in order to join the people of God in their Exodus redemption out of slavery and into the Promised Land. The writer of Hebrews finds him a powerful example for his Christian readers.

Having shown that faith which trusts God enabled believers in the past to obey, be patient and face death, the writer now turns to consider Moses, the stellar giant of Jewish history. In particular, the author stresses that Moses was enabled by his faith to surrender his luxurious life in this world to join the people of God as they endured hardships and suffering in their journey to the kingdom of God.

Moses chose to identify with his Hebrew slave people rather than with his foster family in the palace of Egypt. In three sections, the writer describes how Moses surrendered privileges, endured opposition and prepared for judgement (the first is longer than the others). Such unworldly faith is commended to all Christians today.

## By faith he surrendered privileges! (v 24-26)

> By faith Moses, when he had grown up, refused to be known as the son of Pharaoh's daughter. **(v 24)**

Moses was brought up by Pharaoh's daughter as her own son. In all probability, this was a pharaoh of the 19th dynasty (c.1300 BC), but theories about his identity are speculative. Moses was 'educated in all the wisdom of the Egyptians and was powerful in speech and action' (Acts 7 v 22), an impressive and privileged prince of the Egyptian empire. He could well have nurtured ambitions for government and even the throne. But Moses chose a humbler route.

### *He abandoned his status*

We read in Acts that, when Moses was 40, 'he decided to visit his fellow Israelites. He saw one of them being ill-treated by an Egyptian, so he went to his defence and avenged him by killing the Egyptian' (Acts 7 v 23-24). In starting to visit his own people, Moses was consciously choosing to identify with his slave people rather than with Pharaoh's household and the Egyptian ruling class. Hebrews concludes that he 'refused to be known as the son of Pharaoh's daughter'. He was willing to surrender the status and comforts of a prince of Egypt for the contempt and privations of the people of God. In our culture that adores celebrities and yearns for star status and 15 minutes of fame, such a choice is very challenging. Many men find it hard to risk losing some status in their careers by attending a lunchtime gospel outreach, insisting upon costly ethical principles or refusing to work all hours so that they can be with their families or help out at church.

Moses' decision is reflected in the same priority shown by the legendary C. T. Studd (1860-1931). Having captained the Cambridge and England cricket teams, he appeared to have a glittering career ahead of him. But Studd abandoned his celebrity status in order to labour as a missionary in China and later, India and Africa. Like Moses, he surrendered status and power for the sake of Christ. And we may be required to do the same.

### *He acted in faith*

This surrender of status was 'by faith' because Moses had clearly heard and accepted God's commission to be the deliverer of Israel.

> Moses thought that his own people would realise that God was using him to rescue them … **Acts 7 v 25**

Moses' decision to identify with Israel was not that of a zealous human-rights protester or even of a compassionate, charitable aid-worker. It was costly faith in the commission of God. We too are commissioned by Jesus to 'make disciples of all nations' (Matthew 28) and we shall need to persevere in this charge 'by faith'.

### *He surrendered pleasure*

> He chose to be ill-treated along with the people of God rather than to enjoy the pleasures of sin for a short time **(v 25)**

The writer doesn't clarify which pleasures of sin he is referring to, but the corruptions of power, idolatry and immorality were fairly obvious temptations for Egyptian royalty.

The benefits of political power and high rank are, of course, not necessarily evil. The work over many years of William Wilberforce and others in Parliament to eventually abolish slavery is eloquent testimony to what can be done by God through a Christian of high rank. But for Moses to reject what he knew God wanted of him in order to retain his status would have been sinful. The same could be true today of a Christian man who refused a considered encouragement from his church leaders to pursue full-time gospel ministry and chose instead to continue enjoying his status as the head of department in a school or the manager of a division in a business.

Moses also rejected idolatry. To remain in Pharaoh's palace meant colluding in the pluralistic idolatry of the Egyptian religions. For Moses to know God and yet participate in the paganism of Egypt would have been wicked. The same could be true today of a Christian man who participates in a multi-faith service as if all religions are ways to God.

Moreover, immorality must have been tempting. With his position came ample opportunity for self-indulgence. Egyptian hedonism was legendary. The sexual pleasure of the harems, the material luxury of the palaces and the constant service of the slaves must have been very attractive. But Moses could not know God and continue in such vices. The same is true of Christian men today who must abandon old habits of drinking and visiting strip clubs with their colleagues.

Apparently, catching monkeys is easy! You just put apples coated in syrup into cans or bottles which have openings only slightly larger than the apples and which are then tethered to the ground. If a monkey puts its hand into the bottle or can and closes it around the fruit, it will not then be able to remove its hand while holding onto the apple. Indeed, rather than let go of its delicious prize, it will allow itself to be easily captured. It is trapped by its greed. Tragically, some men are like that, unable to let go of the pleasures they enjoy and so trapped in sin. Moses encourages us all to let go of sin.

### He preferred to be ill-treated with God's people

[Moses] chose to be ill-treated along with the people of God. v 25

This meant choosing the contempt, poverty and slavery of the Hebrews. It was not that Moses wanted ill-treatment but that he wanted to join the people of God. For Christian men in this country today, this may mean facing mockery and contempt for unpopular beliefs, eg: for doctors who refuse to encourage abortions, or builders who refuse to cut corners.

It may soon mean legal prosecution, eg: for teachers who cannot in conscience teach their schoolchildren how to practise homosexuality. In many Muslim and Communist regimes, such ill-treatment may mean physical beatings or intimidation, prejudiced denial of jobs or other opportunities, exclusion from families and communities, or even prison and death.

### He surrendered treasure

> He regarded disgrace for the sake of Christ as of greater value than the treasures of Egypt. **v 26**

The treasures of Egypt are famous. To abandon the opulent comforts of civilised life in his own palatial home for the hovels of the slaves and his exile in Midian must have felt extremely costly. But Moses actually preferred disgrace! 'For the sake of Christ' can be literally translated 'the reproach of the Anointed'. It certainly doesn't mean that Moses knew Christ as Christians now do (the incarnation of Christ, as further revealed in the New Testament to Christians with the help of the indwelling Holy Spirit, means that Christians today know Christ better than Old Testament believers could then have known Him).

The 'Anointed' for whom Moses suffered consciously was the chosen people of God in whom Christ also suffers. Moses actually thought that it was more valuable in the long run to have suffered disgrace for God's people than to possess the treasures of Pharaoh. After all, the pharaohs tried to take their immense fortunes with them into death in their pyramids, but grave robbers took the lot. Moses realised that the honour of suffering disgrace for the people of Christ lasts into eternity.

Such wisdom is similar to that of Eric Liddell, the 'flying Scotsman' of *Chariots of Fire* fame. He played international rugby for Scotland and is even more famous for his sprinting. He won national championships in both 100m and 200m in 1921, 1922 and 1923, and then, in 1924 in Paris, the Olympic 400m gold. But he is most admired for an extraordinary decision that reflected the priorities of Moses. He refused to run in his preferred 100m race at the Olympics because the heats were to be run on a Sunday, and it was his settled conviction that Sunday should be kept special for the Lord. He pulled out of the sprint relays for the same reason and was accused of being a traitor to his country for refusing to compromise his principles.

When Harold Abrahams, whom he'd earlier beaten, went on to win the gold, Eric was preaching the gospel in a church in Paris. Whether or not we think he was right about running on Sundays, can we imagine sacrificing the Olympic gold medal in the 100m, after training so hard to win, for a biblical principle? Like Moses, Liddell preferred the disgrace of serving Christ to the treasures of Olympic gold medals.

Why? What could possibly make a man give up so much?

## He was looking forward to heaven...

...because he was looking ahead to his reward. v 26

Moses saw with the eyes of faith into the future God has prepared for those who love Him. The writer to the Hebrews has explained earlier in this chapter that faith is 'being sure of what we hope for' (v 1). He has given examples such as Abraham longing for a heavenly city and country. Moses couldn't have known much about the kingdom of God. But he somehow knew from God that the deliverance of Israel from slavery in Egypt promised a future reward in the heavenly kingdom, and he valued eternal approval of God more than the trinkets and baubles of Egypt.

I recently climbed with my two oldest children to the top of Mount Snowdon in North Wales. By the standards of serious climbers and walkers this is little more than a stroll, but I found it knackering. On the way up, limbs aching and lungs bursting, I often asked myself why I was doing it (other than to prove some-thing to the kids!). Of course, the motivation was to reach the summit. The views from the top on that sunny day were truly spectacular. The rewards at the end more than made up for the effort and costs of getting there. This is obvious. And it was obvious to Moses and to Eric Liddell. The joys of life with God in His new world will more than make up for the hardships of joining His people in this world.

## By faith he endured opposition!

> By faith he left Egypt, not fearing the king's anger; he persevered because he saw him who is invisible. **v 27**

The order of the events in our passage indicates that the leaving of Egypt being referred to is Moses' departure to live in Midian for 40 years, where 'he settled as a foreigner and had two sons' (Acts 7 v 29).

This leaving was again 'by faith' because, rather than try to raise a slaves' revolt in Egypt or negotiate a reconciliation with Pharaoh, he seems to have left for Midian to await the LORD's will for him to be used in delivering Israel. It was a further 40 years before the LORD finally revealed Himself to Moses in a burning bush on Mount Horeb and instructed him in how to rescue His people. Having been told that he would be Israel's deliverer, Moses did not try either to invent his own way of doing it (not very sensible, given the power of Pharaoh) or to run away from it. He seems to have trusted God to govern his future. Being a Christian often involves faithfully waiting for opportunities for service. We often don't know what to do next. But we must wait, trusting God to make it clear in His good time.

### *He wasn't afraid of the king*

We're told that Moses went 'not fearing the king's anger'. We do read in Exodus that Moses was afraid when he realised that his murder of the Egyptian slave-master was known amongst the

Hebrew slaves. But this was before Moses left Egypt, and the writer of Hebrews wants his readers to recognise that Moses' trust in God removed his fear of the king sufficiently to enable him to leave his home and country. The pharaohs exercised absolute power in Egypt. But, as Moses was to discover in the plagues, Pharaoh was as a piece of straw in the grip of the LORD Almighty, our God.

Faith in God does enable men to do great things for Him by removing their fear. The famous missionary Hudson Taylor's final decision to go to China with the gospel was built upon a trust in God to deal with the immense obstacles and dangers:

> On Sunday, June 25th, 1865, unable to bear the sight of a congregation of a thousand or more Christian people rejoicing in their own security, while millions were perishing for lack of knowledge, I wandered out on the sands alone, in great spiritual agony; and there the Lord conquered my unbelief, and I surrendered myself for this service. I told him that all the responsibility as to issues and consequences must rest with him, that as his servant, it was mine to obey and to follow him – his to direct, to care for and to guide me and those who might labour with me.[1]

How did Hudson Taylor come to such confidence in God as to leave his home for China? How did Moses come to such faith in God as to leave his home for Midian?

### *He saw the invisible God*

He persevered because he saw Him who is invisible.

This verse is not speaking of seeing God in the burning bush (which was 40 years later). It speaks of Moses trusting God without physically seeing Him. Our author has already said that faith is not only being sure of the future we hope for, but also of being certain of things we can't see because God has promised them. Christian men today must be the same. In every frightening situation, we can see, by faith, that God is there.

At that frightening appraisal where my commitment to the company will be questioned because I leave work early for homegroup, God will be sitting beside me. In that discussion with colleagues about the damage religion is doing in the world, God is standing there with me. In that painful conversation with frustrated unbelieving parents about why we plan to live in Africa with their youngest grandchild in order to help at a mission hospital, God will be there. We, like Moses, can persevere in what is right if we will only look around and see that the invisible God is with us. The prophet Elisha, surrounded by an army of chariots, asked to be shown the armies of God in order to reassure his frightened servant: 'Then the LORD opened the servant's eyes, and he looked and saw the hills full of horses and chariots of fire all around Elisha' (2 Kings 6 v 17).

## By faith he prepared for judgment!

> By faith he kept the Passover and the sprinkling of blood, so that the destroyer of the firstborn would not touch the firstborn of Israel. **v28**

It may be helpful briefly to rehearse these historic events.

When Pharaoh repeatedly rejected the LORD's command to let Israel leave Egypt, the LORD finally issued a chilling ultimatum: unless Pharaoh released Israel, the LORD's firstborn son whom Pharaoh had enslaved, the LORD would pass through Egypt in judgement of its idolatrous defiance and kill all the firstborn sons in the land.

But the LORD also provided the means of surviving His judgment. He told Moses to instruct God's people to obtain a flawless male lamb for every family with enough for everyone to eat. Each family would care for its lamb for four days until the night of the 'Passover'. On that night, the lambs must be slaughtered and the blood of the lambs sprinkled around the doors of their houses, indicating that death had already occurred in those houses. Later that night, the LORD would pass through Egypt destroying all firstborn sons except where there had been the death of a lamb in the place of a son. The blood of the substitutionary sacrifice would satisfy the Lord and He would 'Pass over' that house, leaving the Hebrew boys alive.

Pharaoh remained stubborn, and judgment followed as promised. The night this happened was the night Pharaoh finally surrendered to the Lord and let Israel go. It was the beginning of a new life for Israel, redeemed from slavery by the blood of the 'Passover' animal, a day to be celebrated forever in the Promised Land. The meat of that sacrifice and the unleavened bread of hasty departure were to sustain God's people for their journey.

The New Testament clarifies how this momentous deliverance points to the redeeming death of Christ. While the Passover lambs were being sacrificed in the temple of Jerusalem, Jesus, the true 'Passover', was being sacrificed on a cross. His blood satisfied the Lord and diverts the wrath we deserve away from all who paint His blood over their lives.

He bore our hellish death penalty so that we might be spared, leaving the slavery imposed by Satan and journeying to the promised kingdom of God in heaven. Indeed, the death of Jesus sustains us throughout that journey and we celebrate our deliverance with a meal, the 'Lord's Supper', which commemorates our Passover deliverance at the cross.

Moses demonstrated his faith in God in three related ways that night.

### *He believed the warning about the judgment to come*
He kept the Passover precisely because he was convinced that the Lord would come to judge sin. God had already brought many other mighty plagues upon Egypt. The Lord had spoken plainly, just as Christ has spoken plainly about judgment and hell. Christians today must also believe in the coming judgment, even if false teachers scoff at the idea. Recently a senior cleric has called the Bible's teaching that Jesus was the 'penal substitute' for His people (bearing the penalty for what we do wrong) 'repulsive as well as nonsensical. It makes God sound like a psychopath.' This

cleric is denying the plain truth that a loving holy God must punish and destroy the sin and evil that so distorts human life. Men of faith like Moses continue to believe in judgment, even if others surrender to the politically correct demands of this world.

### *He believed the Passover sacrifice to be a 'penal substitutionary satisfaction' of God*

Moses understood that the death of the lamb, like the death of Jesus, was 'penal' (bearing the 'penalty' of our sin) 'substitutionary' (swapping places with sinners just as a football 'substitute' swaps with another player on the pitch) 'satisfaction' (completely 'satisfying' God's justice once and for all).

God didn't pick on some poor innocent third party called Jesus and punish Him for our sin (which would be utterly unjust). Rather, God Himself took flesh in Jesus. God Himself was 'reconciling the world to himself in Christ' (2 Corinthians 5 v 19) by accepting upon Himself the penalty for our sin. God is not three separate gods, with one picking on another, but one God accepting our penalty in Christ's death on the cross because He loves us so passionately.

Let me illustrate. Sergeant Ian Mackay was posthumously awarded the Victoria Cross for his bravery during the historic 'yomp' march during the Falkland Islands' War between the UK and Argentina. Mackay and his men from 3rd Battalion, The Parachute Regiment, found themselves trapped on the side of Mount Longdon under withering fire from a machine-gun position at the top of the hill. It was obvious that few could hope to escape from such an exposed position.

Discarding his rifle, Mackay stood up gripping grenades from his chest webbing, pulled the pins and charged up the hill to blow up the machine-gun post and himself in the process. One can imagine that, as the deafening noise of gunfire, shouting and then explosion echoed across the hills and then subsided into silence, Mackay's men must have gradually realised what he'd done for them. He'd given his life for them. Even if they'd thought little of Mackay before that moment, from that day on they would surely honour his memory in the knowledge that he had died in their place, and would never hear another bad word said about him.

So it is with Christians. The day we realise that Jesus charged up the hill of Calvary to suffer the explosion of God's wrath directed at us, that day we will begin to honour Him as our Saviour. But such sacrifice would be fairly pointless if it didn't save us from the penalty we deserve. When some suggest that Christ was crucified to 'share in the worst of grief and suffering that life can throw at us', it is like suggesting that Sgt Mackay should be honoured because he stood up and got himself shot to know what it felt like! To walk into gunfire for no reason but to share in being shot, is not loving. The reason Christ's death was so loving towards us is that He suffered our penalty.

The words of Isaiah 53 v 5-6 (famous from Handel's Messiah) put it so clearly:

> But he was pierced for our transgressions,
> he was crushed for our iniquities;
> the punishment that brought us peace was upon him,
> and by his wounds we are healed.
> We all, like sheep, have gone astray,
> each of us has turned to his own way;
> and the Lord has laid on him the iniquity of us all.

Moses understood this, so he obeyed God's instructions for the Passover lambs.

### *He believed he had to persuade others to do the same*

He ensured the protection of all the firstborn of Israel. He persuaded all the people to nurture and sacrifice their own lambs. Anyone with faith to understand the way of deliverance from both the last plague of God (and the day of judgment yet to come) and the power of Pharaoh (and the power of Satan today) would do what they could to save others, as Moses did. Christian men today must likewise persuade their families, friends and colleagues to rely on our Passover, Christ, for their deliverance – even when this is completely contrary to the world's confidence that God will never judge our sin.

Moses was unworldly in his faith in three related ways. He surrendered the pleasures and treasures of this world in order to join the people of God on their journey, looking forward to the kingdom of God. He endured opposition because he could see what this world cannot see: that human power is subject to the invisible God. And he prepared for the judgment of God by relying, and persuading others to rely, upon the sacrificial lamb.

For his challenging unworldliness, Moses plainly belongs among 'a few good men'.

# BIBLE BACKGROUND

## *Hebrews*

The book of Hebrews was written by an unknown learned church pastor. It is a careful sermon expounding a series of Old Testament passages for some struggling Jewish Christians he loved dearly. They were tempted to drift away, harden their hearts and shrink back from public faith in Christ. They had previously stood firm for Christ in the face of hostile opposition, but were now wearying of the costs of openly following Jesus. So the author wrote to remind them that God has spoken fully, finally and personally to us in these last days by His Son. This Son, Jesus, is a better Prophet, Priest and King, offering a better covenant, priesthood and sacrifice, than anything even in their Jewish history. These Christians needed to persevere in their faith in the gospel promise. We all need to learn, he writes, 'to fix our eyes on Jesus' (12 v 2).

## *Chapter 11*

The author clearly wrote this famous chapter to encourage his readers to keep going. Or, as Winston Churchill apparently brilliantly put it in an extraordinarily short school prize-day speech, to 'Never, never, never give up!'

The chapter is all about living 'by faith'. I recall learning about the importance of faith while I was washing dishes! I had arrived in Sydney, Australia, to study at Moore College and the then Principal, Dr Peter Jensen, kindly picked me up from the airport and took me home for supper. After the meal, I thought I'd better offer to wash up, but as I did so the Principal decided to assess what I knew. He asked me a simple, searching question: 'Richard, what word would you say summarises the Christian life?'

Well, I was drowning. I tried a few suggestions, but he looked more and more depressed. But he didn't put me out of my misery. He kept asking for what seemed like ages, until finally he said quietly, in despair: 'It's 'faith'!' I was humiliated, but I learned a profound lesson. The Christian life is essentially one of faith in God's gospel. The readers of Hebrews needed to realise that for themselves.

The writer defines faith in 11 v 1 as 'being sure of what we hope for and certain of what we don't see'. He wants his readers to understand that normal Christian faith is believing what is promised by the Word of God about the future and about God who is unseen, without yet experiencing what is promised. He lists many Old Testament believers to show that such faith is what God has always required, even of their Jewish ancestors. He lists so many examples that this chapter is not, as many claim, a 'Hall of Fame' of heroes. In fact, it is hard to think of anyone from the Old Testament who is not listed in it! This faith is not special, but ordinary and normal to all believers. 'All these people were still living by faith when they died. They did not receive the things promised; they only saw them and welcomed them from a distance ... These were all commended for their faith, yet none of them received what had been promised' (v 13, 39).

He begins each example with 'By faith', to show that their faith resourced their actions, particularly in perseverance and endurance through trials and opposition. Moreover, he encourages his readers by reminding them that such faith was commended by God even in otherwise unimpressive people.

## Questions for group discussion

1. What do we find surprising about the Bible's attitude to this world?
2. What status, pleasures and treasures do Christians have to surrender today?
3. Do we find it hard to be sure of what we hope for, and certain of what we don't see?

### References
1 Marshall Broomhall, *Hudson Taylor: The man who believed God*, CIM and RTS, 1929, p.117.

# 5 WHOLEHEARTED CALEB

*'I, however, followed the* LORD *my God wholeheartedly'*

JOSHUA 14 V 8

hristians are often dismissed as being weak and wimpy. In *The Simpsons*, the Christian, Ned Flanders, is painfully pathetic. The caricatures of Christian clergy in *Father Ted*, *Mr Bean* and *Four Weddings and a Funeral* are all hopelessly inadequate. The most compelling is found in *The Vicar of Dibley* and she's a woman! The truth is that the gospel of Christ calls men to follow into spiritual battle. Like Jesus we must be humble, but far from weak or spineless. We want to be clearly distinct from the violence of Christian fanaticism, but we are called to be warriors in a vicious spiritual war. In this conflict, we have much to learn from the hardened veteran soldier, Caleb.

We fight, not with Canaanite tribes, but against the world, the flesh and the devil. We must demolish the arguments of the world around us with the spiritual weapons of gospel truth (2 Corinthians 10). We must kill off the misdeeds of our sinful flesh in the Holy Spirit's assurance of the gospel (Romans 8). We must stand up to the spiritual forces of Satan in the armour of gospel convictions (Ephesians 6 v 10-18).

Caleb is an example of fighting these battles with wholehearted faith in God. Three times in Joshua 14 v 6-15 we are told that Caleb followed the LORD 'wholeheartedly' (lit. 'completely' – v 8, 9, 14). His faith in God's promise of an inheritance in His earthly kingdom gave him courage to fight for that inheritance long after most men retire to play golf. God arranged for this stirring account to inspire not only the next generation of Israelites, but also Christians today who must 'fight the good fight of the faith' (1 Timothy 6 v 12). Caleb teaches us how to fight 'wholeheartedly'. This man was a hero, a legend, a warrior: a real man's man of faith.

> Now the men of Judah approached Joshua at Gilgal, and Caleb son of Jephunneh the Kenizzite said to him, 'You know what the LORD said to Moses the man of God at Kadesh Barnea about you and me. I was forty years old when Moses the servant of the LORD sent me from Kadesh Barnea to explore the land. And I brought him back a report according to my convictions, but my brothers who went up with me made the hearts of the people sink. I, however, followed the LORD my God wholeheartedly. So on that day Moses swore to me, 'The land on which your feet have walked will be your inheritance and that of your children for ever, because you have followed the LORD my God wholeheartedly.'

> 'Now then, just as the LORD promised, he has kept me alive for forty-five years since the time he said this to Moses, while Israel moved about in the desert. So here I am today, eighty-five years old! I am still as strong today as the day Moses sent me out; I'm just as vigorous to go out to battle now as I was then. Now give me this hill country that the LORD promised me that day. You yourself heard then that the Anakites were there and their cities were large and fortified, but, the LORD helping me, I will drive them out just as he said.'

> Then Joshua blessed Caleb son of Jephunneh and gave him Hebron as his inheritance. So Hebron has belonged to Caleb son of Jephunneh the Kenizzite ever since, because he followed the LORD, the God of Israel, wholeheartedly. (Hebron used to be called Kiriath Arba after Arba, who was the greatest man among the Anakites.)

> Then the land had rest from war. **Joshua 14 v 6-15**

*The battle-hardened warriors of Judah had gathered outside Joshua's tent at Gilgal, by the Jordan River. This famous site of the miraculous Israelite crossing into Canaan had been Joshua's military base for the last seven years of ferocious warfare. But one* man among the troops was noticeably different from the rest. Caleb was 85 years old.

He and Joshua were the only survivors of their generation. They were the only men alive who could still remember the nightmare of Egyptian slavery, before the hardship of the great desert trek. They'd buried all their contemporaries in the Sinai desert and many more in the battles for Canaan. Now the great veteran chief had come to talk with his old friend and commander, Joshua, about one final campaign. The younger men must have sensed the mutual respect and affection between these two living legends as they embraced. Surely they listened intently as Caleb spoke of epic events from the past.

Caleb proceeded to remind Joshua of the tragic rebellion of Israel 45 years earlier at Kadesh Barnea on the southern borders of the Promised Land. After two years at Mount Sinai receiving the Word of God, the nomadic mass of redeemed but rebellious Israelites had arrived at the borders of Canaan full of hope. Moses had sent 12 Israelite leaders to reconnoitre the situation, among them Joshua and Caleb. When they returned, all the spies were in agreement: the land was indeed beautiful, a paradise of mountain streams, olive groves and coastal luxury. But there were also powerful and hostile enemies. Only Caleb and Joshua had retained their faith in the LORD to give them this land.

That night the Israelites had complained bitterly and discussed returning to Egypt. Caleb and Joshua, deeply distressed by such loss of faith in God, had stood up and appealed to the crowd: 'Do not rebel against the LORD. And do not be afraid of the people of the land, because we will swallow them up. Their protection is gone but the LORD is with us. Do not be afraid of them.' But the Israelite assembly had threatened to stone Caleb and Joshua to death. They hated such zealous confidence in God. In their panic, they'd quickly forgotten the power of the LORD displayed in the plagues and exodus from Egypt, at Mount Sinai and on the journey.

*Such pious talk seemed ridiculous, even dangerous. It was contrary to all human logic. They could never hope to conquer Canaan.*

*But the LORD had heard the whole wretched business. Caleb and Joshua had been vindicated by God, but all the rest of that generation had been condemned to die in the wilderness. And Caleb had been promised by God an inheritance in the beautiful region of Hebron, where he'd walked.*

*Since that time, 45 years had elapsed. Caleb and Joshua could both remember those epic years in the desert. Plagues, battles and rebellions. And then, after many years, the final gathering took place in the plains of Moab, east of the Jordan, where Moses had preached his final three sermons before dying. And for the last seven years, the ferocious campaigns in Canaan. Jericho was but a distant memory now. So much bloodshed and bravery, too. But now Caleb was determined to receive his own inheritance. He had followed Joshua with great loyalty and distinction all these years. But now he spoke with conviction not to be refused. 'So here I am today, eighty-five years old! I am still as strong today as the day Moses sent me out,' he claimed with deliberate exaggeration. The troops around him cheered their support for their grizzly old general, whose arms and eyesight were not as strong as they had once been. But now the soldiers were stilled by the serious note in his voice. 'Now give me this hill country that the LORD promised me that day'.*

*Caleb could not be refused, even by Joshua. All the soldiers could hear that Caleb had the word of the LORD Himself as his authority. Even Joshua must accede to this request. Referring to the Anakite armies, Caleb finished with an inspiring flourish. 'The LORD helping me, I will drive them out,' he exclaimed, as he turned to his troops for their support. He was not disappointed, for the men cheered with one voice, showing their willingness to fight for this great man of faith. When the cheering subsided, Joshua smiled with approval and reassurance. He blessed Caleb and granted Hebron to him. The man who followed the LORD whole-heartedly would be honoured. Surely God had kept his promise and rewarded wholehearted faith.*

---

## Wholehearted faith in God's promise took away his fear! (v 6-10)

Caleb's confidence was not just an optimistic outlook that assumes everything will work out well. It often doesn't. Nor was it a confidence that God will give us whatever we want 'if we just have enough faith'. That isn't true. Rather, Caleb's confidence was in the LORD's faithfulness to honour His promise to Abraham of an inheritance in the kingdom of God (Genesis 12 v 1-3); it was confidence in the gospel. This faith had dissolved away any fear he had of the opposition.

### *His faith was trust in the word of God (v 6)*

Caleb began his appeal to Joshua with the words: 'You know what the LORD said ...' He would refer to this promise repeatedly (v 9, 10, 12). Caleb's faith wasn't optimism or bravery. Caleb trusted the LORD to keep His word and overcome all obstacles and opposition. After all, even His name 'LORD' (meaning 'I am who I am') emphasised His sovereign freedom to be faithful to His own promises.

Likewise, we can trust this same LORD, who in the gospel of Christ has promised us an eternal inheritance in His heavenly kingdom. As Paul later put it: 'I am convinced that neither death nor life, neither angels nor demons, neither the present nor the future, nor any powers, neither height nor depth, nor anything else in all creation, will be able to separate us from the love of God that is in Christ Jesus our Lord' (Romans 8 v 38-39). The LORD makes other promises in Scripture and He is equally to be trusted with them, too. Like Caleb, we can take Him at His word. Perhaps the old practice of starting a prayer with a promise from Scripture should be revived.

This was the faith of a Christian young man who died recently of a brain tumour. He came to see me a few months ago to say goodbye and pray before he died. He was pale and weak. He was deeply sad to be leaving his wife and family and friends behind. But his eyes were bright with quiet confidence in the gospel promise and looking forward to being with Jesus. That is Caleb's faith: trust in the word of God.

### His faith altered his view of the opposition (v 7)

When Caleb and the other spies were sent to reconnoitre Canaan, they all saw the same beautiful land with the same powerful warriors and the same impregnable walled cities. But they reported quite differently! Most described how it appeared superficially. But Caleb reported 'according to my convictions' (lit. 'as in my heart'), seeing the opposition in the light of God's promise.

Likewise today, we face powerful enemies ranged against us. Our western world is increasingly hostile to God. Materialism has given birth to a hedonism that welcomes late-night drinking, casinos and brothels, and promotes the pursuit of fine cuisine, luxury homes and holidays in paradise. Secularism has spawned the suppression of Christianity, so that best-selling novels like Dan Brown's *Da Vinci Code* mock the historicity of the Bible. Atheistic scientists like Richard Dawkins arrogantly proclaim God to be a delusion of our mental illness, and things like *Jerry Springer: The Opera* are considered great entertainment!

The world is certainly a powerful enemy. Our own flesh is worse. Our sinful nature tempts us to all manner of selfish idolatries, ranging from the envy and anger of selfish ambition to drooling lust for designer shirts and Internet porn. Just when we think we have weeded out one idol that displaces God in our affections, ten more soon sprout up in its place. Our own flesh is a powerful obstacle. Most terrifying of all is Satan himself. He promotes false teaching, uses our suffering to suggest that God doesn't care and undermines unity in the gospel. He peddles his ancient lies about sin: 'You will not surely die [God wouldn't really send anyone to hell] ... Did God really say ...? [You can't be sure what God's Word says.] ... God knows ... your eyes will be opened [God is inhibiting your maturity]' (Genesis 3). The world, the flesh and the devil are indeed a frightening tag team seeking to wrestle our inheritance from us. But the almighty LORD of heaven and earth has promised to take us home to heaven and He won't fail those who trust in Him.

I once asked a Palestinian Christian friend living in Jerusalem whether he was scared. Caught between the Israeli soldiers and the Muslim imams he was in great danger. But he simply and firmly replied: 'Our Father's in charge so I'm not worried.' That's Caleb's faith. We have nothing to fear from the world, the flesh and the devil. The opposition won't seem so scary when we look at it with Caleb's faith, however weak and wicked we may feel or look to others.

### *His faith enabled him to stand against the crowd (v 8)*

Caleb recalled that the faithless spies had made the hearts of the people 'sink' with fear (lit. 'melt', v 8) as they described the powerful Anakite warriors (descended from the evil and terrifying giant 'Nephilim') and their strongly fortified cities. 'We seemed like grasshoppers in our own eyes,' they'd said (Numbers 13 v 33). They'd felt so pathetic compared with the enemy – like a primary schoolboy rugby team taking on the mighty All Blacks! But Caleb had seen it differently: 'We should go up and take possession of the land, for we can certainly do it' (Numbers 13 v 30).

Caleb knew that faith in God's gospel promise forced him to stand apart from everyone else, criticised, unpopular and threatened. We can expect the same today. The man who invites his colleagues to a lunchtime Bible talk can expect to be scorned. The man who conducts his business with scrupulous integrity can expect to be criticised. The man on a business jolly who refuses to go with colleagues to a strip bar can expect to find himself isolated. The man who refuses to misrepresent his firm's failures towards a client can expect to be sidelined. And the unbelievers may well be in the church: 'We can't possibly plan a mission – it would upset our delicate relations with the local community!' 'We certainly can't attempt to plant a new church – we'd never be allowed by the diocese!' 'And don't you dare visit our MP to contend for freedom to preach the gospel – our reputation will be ruined!'

Some of the fiercest opposition will come from those who should know better, even the pastors and bishops. We need to pray for our leaders to discover the faith of Caleb and to stand up for the gospel in the House of Lords or at denominational meetings. Faith in the gospel will often require us to stand against the crowd as Caleb did. But it will be worth it in the end.

### His faith was rewarded by God (v 9)

The LORD had heard and seen everything. While His wrath had burned towards the contemptuous Israelites, He had graciously promised blessing to faithful Caleb:

> Not one of them will ever see the land I promised on oath to their forefathers. No one who has treated me with contempt will ever see it. But because my servant Caleb has a different spirit and follows me wholeheartedly, I will bring him into the land he went to, and his descendants will inherit it. **Numbers 14 v 23-24**

We do need to realise that Caleb's faith is not optional. If we will not trust God's Word, we are treating Him with contempt and cannot expect any inheritance in His kingdom. But if we have the 'different spirit' of confidence in God and His Word, we too can look forward to an inheritance in the new creation paradise.

It was so appropriate that Caleb was given 'the land on which your feet have walked' (Joshua 4 v 9). It would be a constant reminder all his days that the very land which everyone else thought it was impossible to occupy was now his. Nothing and no one can stop the LORD keeping His promises. And what a joy it will be for us to hear the voice of God one day soon in heaven, inviting us to gaze out at the beautiful land of our inheritance! He'll show us around the many rooms that Jesus went to prepare. We'll hear Him solemnly and publicly declare to each of us these words which we will treasure forever: 'because you have followed the LORD your God wholeheartedly.'

But in verses 10-12, Caleb stops reminding Joshua of the past and comes to the present. Since Kadesh Barnea, 45 years had elapsed. We know that Caleb continued as a chief in his clan. Indeed, when the LORD told Moses to choose leaders to help Joshua and Eleazar distribute the Promised Land to Israel, Caleb was honoured with being first on the list (Numbers 34 v 19). But those years had been very hard...

### His faith enabled him to wait (v 10)

Caleb had spent the last 45 years waiting. Waiting for all of his contemporaries but Joshua to die. So many funerals! Waiting in faith. As the years rolled by and his generation thinned out, it must have become more and more apparent that the LORD was simply delaying their entry to Canaan until His promise of judgement was fulfilled. For God keeps His promise to punish every bit as faithfully as His promise to bless! It must have been difficult not to resent the faithlessness of the others as he was forced to wait, even harder knowing that his friends and wider family were not to be there with him. Likewise, our response to the gospel is no trivial attitude. It still determines our eternity.

And then came the wars: Jericho, Ai and the rest. The whole country was soaked in the blood of the tribes who defied the rule of the LORD. All that time waiting for the promised blessing. Thirty eight years in slavery crying out for deliverance; forty years in the desert struggling to survive; seven years in Canaan fighting to take the inheritance. When would the blessings ever arrive? It can feel like that for Christians, too. Although knowing God as our Father makes all of life better, our Christian life is essentially one of waiting in faith. Paul says to the Thessalonian Christians: 'You turned to God from idols to serve the living and true God, and to wait for his Son from heaven' (1 Thessalonians 1 v 9-10). Truly, God has 'blessed us in the heavenly realms with every spiritual blessing in Christ' (Ephesians 1 v 3), but we are not yet in heaven. And so we must wait, patiently (or, as Take That sing it, *'Have a little patience'!*).

But now, for Caleb, the long waiting of faith was nearly over. After all those years, it was now time for him and the tribe of Judah to take their own inheritance in the luscious regions south and west of Jerusalem.

## Wholehearted faith in God's promise made him willing to fight! (v 10-12)

Caleb's faith had dissolved away fear and replaced it with the courage to fight for his inheritance.

### *His faith recognised the LORD's faithfulness (v 10)*

Caleb preceded his declaration of confidence for the future with a reflection upon the LORD's faithfulness to him over many years: 'Just as [He] promised, He has kept me alive for forty-five years' (v 10). It must have been so tempting to foster the adulation of the younger troops by attributing his survival to his own skills in desert warfare.

But Caleb knew that the only reason he and Joshua were still alive was because of the sustaining power of God in keeping His promise. We have much to learn from him. Men with Caleb's faith are quick to attribute the growth of their businesses, the health of their families, the growth of their churches and the influence of their ministries not to themselves, but to the LORD's faithfulness.

### *His faith made him ready to fight for the LORD (v 11)*

One can imagine the younger warriors roaring with affectionate laughter as the wizened old general waved his walking stick in defiance. 'So here I am today, eighty-five years old! I am still as strong today as the day Moses sent me out; I'm just as vigorous to go out to battle now as I was then' (v 10-11). This veteran wasn't looking to fade away in retirement. He wasn't about to waste his last years down the bowling club, or in front of Sky Sports, or up at the garden centre or painting his seaside holiday cottage! Even if his body was weakening, his zeal for the work of the LORD burned as brightly in his eyes as it had ever done.

I can think of men like this. For example, David, who retired from teaching in a top boy's school and began an 'apprenticeship' learning gospel ministry. Refreshed and equipped, he has just accepted a post as pastor to a small congregation that needs his teaching ministry. At the age of 63, he's full of the spirit of Caleb. In our youth-dominated culture, too many retired Christians think that they are past their 'best-before' date when it comes to serving God. Caleb spent his retirement leading a band of battle-hardened warriors on a glorious mission for almighty God. That's the way to finish well. To 'go out in a blaze of glory' for Christ, not rotting on a cruise ship in the Med.!

### *His faith provided the ambition of his life (v 12)*

Caleb was determined to receive what he had been promised: 'Now give me this hill country that the LORD promised me that day.' The 'hill country' of Hebron was not only beautiful but significant in the history of God's people. The great patriarchs, Abraham (and Sarah), Isaac and Jacob were buried there in the cave of Machpelah in the field near Mamre, which Abraham had bought from the Hittites. To an Israelite, being given the region of Hebron was similar to an Englishman being given Westminster Abbey! And he'd longed for it all his life.

Men with the faith of Caleb make heaven the longing of their life, too. They marry and have children to share the hope of heaven. They squeeze onto the train to work each day in hope of sharing their hope of heaven. They choose where to live, how to spend their money and what to do with their leisure time according to how they'll be able to share the hope of heaven. Such men are driven not by selfish ambition but by gospel ambition. The meaning of life is not travelling this world, but arriving in heaven with as many friends and family in the back seats as possible! Paradoxically, this ambition for heaven is what most enriches life in this world. Caleb's faith provided the ambition of his life.

### His faith made him welcome a challenge (v 12)

Being confident in God, Caleb welcomed the toughest challenge of all: 'You yourself heard then that the Anakites were there and their cities were large and fortified, but, the LORD helping me, I will drive them out just as he said.' The cities of that region were indeed huge, 'with walls up to the sky' (Deuteronomy 1 v 28). But if God had promised it to him, Caleb reasoned, his victory would be all the more rewarding. He could do it because of the strength of God. He says: 'The LORD helping me, I will drive them out, just as he said' (the original includes the word 'perhaps', not indicating doubt in God, but humility because he is in God's hands). Caleb wasn't stupid. He knew he was just a frail old man. But with the living LORD, the sovereign Creator and Ruler of all, to strengthen him, nothing was beyond him. Just like 45 years earlier at Kadesh Barnea, Caleb was now seeing the obstacles through the eyes of faith. What others would think was an obstacle, Caleb regarded as an opportunity.

The story is told of a shoe company sending a young salesman to West Africa to explore the possibility of opening up a new market. The young salesman sadly discovered that no one wore shoes in West Africa, and so reported: 'No sales possible as no one here wears shoes at all. Bring me home!' A second salesman followed and saw the situation somewhat differently. He e-mailed the central office: 'Send all the shoes you have as no one here wears shoes at all so endless sales opportunities.' In the same way, a man with Caleb's faith will see opposition to the people of God as wonderful opportunities for God to glorify Himself. The threats of extremist Muslim societies, the indifference of atheistic colleagues, the obstructions of liberal bishops – all are opportunities to witness the power of God. What we need is 'not great faith in God but faith in a great God'!

## Wholehearted faith in God's promise proved to be worthwhile! (v 13-15)

It all turned out just as the LORD promised. Joshua blessed his old friend Caleb and gave him Hebron, just as our 'Joshua' will give us our inheritance one day. We read in Judges 1 that after capturing Jerusalem, the men of Judah 'advanced against the Canaanites living in Hebron (formerly called Kiriath Arba) and defeated Sheshai, Ahiman and Talmai ... As Moses had promised, Hebron was given to Caleb, who drove from it the three sons of Anak' (Judges 1 v 10, 20).

Caleb and the warriors of Judah and Simeon proceeded to sweep all before them as they captured the opulent coastal cities. We know that the town of Hebron itself was given to the descendents of Aaron the priest, but 'the fields and villages around the city they had given to Caleb' (Joshua 21 v 12). Caleb was further honoured in having his daughter Acsah marry Othniel (his famous young nephew), who would be the first great 'judge' (spirit-filled warrior-deliverer) and who governed for 40 years and overpowered the Aramites, restoring peace to Israel (Judges 3 v 7-11). It's striking that, because Caleb wanted Acsah to marry someone of his own faith, he offered her hand to whomever would capture a city for the LORD, and Othniel won the prize – though we're not told what Acsah thought of this idea (Judges 1 v 12-13). It is also noticeable that Caleb later very generously gave well-watered land to his son-in law. No doubt he was conscious of God's generosity to him.

Caleb outlasted Joshua to become the only surviving veteran of his generation to enjoy living in peace in his inheritance for many years with his family. They must have become a very distinguished family indeed, regaled at mealtimes by the old general Caleb and the young champion Othniel with marvellous tales of battles and leaders. And especially about the grace and power of God. And all because Caleb followed the LORD wholeheartedly (v 14). Isn't that the kind of family gathering we want to have? When the clan gathers for Christmas, a baptism or a funeral, don't we want to tell stories of what God has been doing in the battles we face?

How dull to have no tales of valour, nothing to say about God to our sons. We need to create our own stories by enlisting for battle with Christ. We need to step out in wholehearted confidence in the LORD. We need to volunteer for the door-to-door visiting, the holiday club, helping with the mission-supporting roles, however daunting they seem. We need to review the fight with this world, the flesh and the devil. And one day, when we're seated in heaven at the LORD's banquet table, perhaps after Caleb has finished, we'll have our own story of wholehearted faith to tell.

The very best bit of all is in the brackets in verse 15: 'Hebron used to be called Kiriath Arba after Arba, who was the greatest man among the Anakites.' These words were needed because no one had heard of Arba any more. Before the people of God arrived, Arba was famous – the greatest warrior of the region: Arnold Schwarzenegger, Vin Diesel and Daniel Craig all rolled into one. But no one knew or cared who he was once Caleb arrived. It was Hebron now, the inheritance of Caleb, the man who followed the LORD wholeheartedly.

For his wholehearted confidence in God, Caleb belongs among 'a few good men'.

## BIBLE BACKGROUND

### *The Bible*

The Scriptures reveal God's promise of an inheritance in the coming kingdom of God through Jesus Christ – the gospel. The Old Testament helps us to understand this gospel promise by recounting how God kept His ancient promise to Abraham of a place for his descendants in the kingdom of God on earth – the land of Canaan (Genesis 12). God nurtured his family into a nation (Genesis). He redeemed them from slavery in Egypt to worship him (Exodus). He provided His law and sacrificial system to enable them to live in His presence (Leviticus). He endured years of rebellion as His people wandered in the desert (Numbers).

He then gathered them in Moab, east of the Promised Land, to republish his law for the new generation (Deuteronomy). The next book, Joshua, records how God finally kept His promise to Abraham and gave Israel an inheritance in the prosperous land of Canaan. God has provided the book of Joshua to reassure Christians today that He will keep His gospel promise to us, just as He did for Israel.

### *Joshua*

The book is constructed in four sections:

- **Entering the land (ch 1-4)** – following Joshua (Jesus), believing the promise, like Rahab, and by God's miraculous power being transferred across the Jordan River into His kingdom. This enlarges our understanding of salvation: of following Jesus, believing in the gospel and the miraculous new birth into the kingdom of God's Son.
- **Taking the land (ch 5-12)** – fighting under the Lord's commander, as at Jericho, obediently, aggressively and humbly, giving all the spoils of victory to the Lord alone. We learn that Christians must fight the good fight of faith with obedience and aggression against the unbelief of the world, the sin of our own flesh and the schemes of the devil, giving all the glory to the Lord for our victorious march towards heaven.
- **Inheriting the land (ch 13-21)** – receiving the allotments, of different towns and areas in the fertile land of Canaan, made by Joshua to each of the tribes of Israel. This enlarges our understanding of that joyful day when our Captain, Jesus, will allot to each of us our eternal inheritance which can never perish, spoil or fade, and which is kept in heaven for us.
- **Keeping the land (ch 22-24)** – restoring those who wandered from the

Lord, carefully obeying the law of God, and throwing away idols in order to serve the Lord. Joshua was himself buried in his promised inheritance. We learn that to keep our inheritance in the kingdom of heaven, God graciously gives us a church family to restore us to faith, the law of Christ by which to live and the call to repentance from worshipping idols, that we too may be buried in the sure and certain hope of resurrection to our eternal inheritance in heaven. God has included the account of Caleb to help Christians understand what kind of faith is required to receive an inheritance in His wonderful kingdom of heaven.

### Chapter 14

This begins a section ending in chapter 19 that describes the inheritance granted to the tribes west of the Jordan river. This section begins with special attention to Caleb and ends with attention to Joshua, for these were the two faithful men who had earlier explored the land under Moses. It emphasises that those who serve the LORD faithfully will surely be honoured on the Day of the Lord Jesus.

Chapter 14 also begins a little section ending in chapter 17 that deals with the allotment of land to the tribes of Judah and Joseph. It seems deliberately to contrast the faithful confidence of Caleb at the beginning with the faithless fear of the tribe of Joseph at the end. This serves to highlight the kind of fighting faith that our Lord wants to find in us. It helps us to understand not only what God wants of men today, but also supremely the kind of faith shown by Jesus Christ as He lived the perfect life of faith that God accepts as ours – the faith of wholehearted Caleb.

## Questions for group discussion

1. How can we learn to see our problems in the light of our convictions?

2. What does it mean for us to serve the LORD wholeheartedly?

3. What are the struggles we face in the fight of faith?

# 6 HUMBLE ISAIAH

*'My eyes have seen the King, the* LORD *Almighty'*

ISAIAH 6 v 5

**H**umility is less admired than it once was. We quite like the brash confidence of youth and the assertive arrogance of genius. When a rock musician claims to be more famous than Jesus, or a football manager says he's the special one, we just smile indulgently. A recent *Sunday Times* article was entitled: 'Generation Y speaks: it's all me, me, me'. The article observed:

> 'The latest generation of graduates – Generation Y – shows the most extreme traits of self-absorption ... Baby boomers and members of Generation X were like dogs – treat them right and they will be loyal. But members of this latest generation, Generation Y, are more like cats: they just go where the money is.'[1]

But becoming a Christian involves a 'Copernican revolution'. Until the 16th century, western thinkers believed the astronomical theories of Ptolemy of Alexandria, that the earth was a fixed mass located at the centre of the universe, around which revolved all celestial bodies. This theory flattered the human ego by seeming to confirm our fondest illusion that we are the centre of the universe.

However, in 1543, Nicolaus Copernicus of Frauenberg Cathedral in Germany published his explosive theory that the earth rotates daily upon its own axis and around the sun once a year. This was a colossal reversal of perspective. It established that the universe does not revolve around us, but that we revolve around the sun. Any requirement to turn one's thinking upside down is now described as a 'Copernican revolution' after this shattering discovery.

When we become a Christian, we discover that God does not live in our universe, revolving around our plans and will. The opposite is the case. We live in His world, revolving around His plans and will. This too is truly a colossal reversal in perspective. Becoming a Christian is a profoundly humbling 'Copernican revolution'.

Indeed, genuine worship and service of God originates in humility, an understanding of our lowly position before God. The great prophet Isaiah was shown something of the holiness of God, and it so humbled him that he became the willing messenger God wanted him to be. We have much to learn from his humbling.

> In the year that King Uzziah died, I saw the Lord seated on a throne, high and exalted, and the train of his robe filled the temple. Above him were seraphs, each with six wings: With two wings they covered their faces, with two they covered their feet, and with two they were flying. And they were calling to one another:
>
> 'Holy, holy, holy is the LORD Almighty;
> the whole earth is full of his glory.'
>
> At the sound of their voices the doorposts and thresholds shook and the temple was filled with smoke.
>
> 'Woe to me!' I cried. 'I am ruined! For I am a man of unclean lips, and I live among a people of unclean lips, and my eyes have seen the King, the LORD Almighty.'
>
> Then one of the seraphs flew to me with a live coal in his hand, which he had taken with tongs from the altar. With it he touched my mouth and said, 'See, this has touched your lips; your guilt is taken away and your sin atoned for.'
>
> Then I heard the voice of the Lord saying, 'Whom shall I send? And who will go for us?'
>
> And I said, 'Here am I. Send me!'
>
> He said, 'Go and tell this people:

'"Be ever hearing, but never understanding;
be ever seeing, but never perceiving."
Make the heart of this people calloused;
make their ears dull
and close their eyes.
Otherwise they might see with their eyes,
hear with their ears,
understand with their hearts,
and turn and be healed.'

Then I said, 'For how long, O Lord?'

And he answered:
'Until the cities lie ruined
and without inhabitant,
until the houses are left deserted
and the fields ruined and ravaged,
until the LORD has sent everyone far away
and the land is utterly forsaken.
And though a tenth remains in the land,
it will again be laid waste.
But as the terebinth and oak
leave stumps when they are cut down,
so the holy seed will be the stump in the land.'

**Isaiah 6 v 1-13**

*Bowed low in silent prayer within the Court of the Israelites in Solomon's temple, Isaiah poured out his heart to the LORD. The nation of Israel (now shrunk to the southern tribes of Judah) had become so prosperous and yet so godless, too. This court used to be filled with men at prayer, but no longer. They were now too busy to pray. Their houses and businesses and trips to the coast left no time for the LORD. Even as the king lay dying and the future so uncertain, no one turned to the LORD.*

*Since coming to the throne at 16, King Uzziah had done much for Judah. Instructed in the fear of God by the prophet Zechariah, he had initially enjoyed many triumphs. He'd defeated the*

Philistines, Arabs and Meunites. He'd rebuilt towns, strengthened Jerusalem, developed a powerful army of 307,000 troops and become famous as a major player in the region. But during these 52 years, Judah had also increasingly abandoned the Word of God. The emerging elite were greedily buying up property. Drunken debauchery was now commonplace in all the towns. Educated society was promoting idolatrous pluralism. An arrogant liberal philosophy that flouted God's laws had captured the schools. And corruption was increasing in government.

More recently, proud Uzziah himself had been struck down with leprosy and forced to live in seclusion. Most believers recognised that this was God's judgment upon his dreadfully arrogant attempt to burn incense in the temple, despite not being a priest of the LORD. Isaiah was grieved as he contemplated the unholy secularism gripping the nation, and cried out to the LORD for mercy and revival.

Suddenly, Isaiah became overwhelmed by a vision of God. Transported in his mind into the Most Holy Place in the temple, where only high priests could enter, he saw in this vision, enthroned above the atonement cover of the ark of the covenant, an immense manifestation of the living God.

It was utterly terrifying.

In this vision, the LORD was seated for sovereign judgment upon a throne. He was high and exalted, clearly ruling with absolute and unrivalled power, untroubled by the petty rebellions of men. Even when seated, His robe completely filled the temple, more than 9 metres high. Here was the LORD, Creator, Redeemer and Judge of all the earth, in magnificent splendour. Uzziah may been dying, but the King of kings still reigned. How could Uzziah have dared to invade this palace-dwelling of the LORD? His effrontery was typical of the nation's pride. Isaiah was utterly overcome by the intimidating magnificence of God, where heaven seemed to be touching the earth.

*And around the throne were countless 'seraphs', awesome heavenly creatures living in the white furnace of God's presence, inflamed with His burning holiness. With two wings they covered their faces in reverent fear of Almighty God. With two more wings they covered their feet out of shame and disgrace before the righteous purity of the LORD. With a further two wings they were effortlessly hovering, ready to perform the LORD's bidding without question.*

*And their praises were marvellous and deafening. Permanently consumed with wonder at God's holiness, they sang in everlasting praise: 'Holy, holy, holy is the LORD Almighty'. They were permanently amazed by His transcendent righteousness. 'The whole earth is full of your glory,' they sang. Isaiah realised that not only the galaxies and oceans, the mountains, forests and deserts of the earth, but also the great cities, technology, art and history of human civilisations, all sing of the glory of God their Creator and sustainer. This heavenly choir was so deafening that the temple itself was shaken as if by an earthquake. And the temple was filled with the smoke of grain and animal offerings sacrificed in homage to him. This smoke was now employed as the Shekinah cloud of protection from the consuming fire of God's holiness. Isaiah was devastated by this vision, crushed to the core of his being by the holiness of the LORD, whom he and his people had disobeyed and disregarded.*

*Drowning in a sense of hopelessness, a deeply corrupt sinner in the presence of Almighty God, Isaiah collapsed in trauma before the LORD. Hardly able to breathe, he cried out in horror: 'Woe to me! I am ruined!' He knew that punishment was imminent. He could see that his moral filthiness deserved nothing less. He had no right even to speak, as the seraphs could speak, in praise of God. 'I am a man of unclean lips, and I live among a people of unclean lips,' he gasped in confession. It was obvious that he could not survive in the presence of this LORD, as foul and offensive to God as he was. And there was no way to improve – this was no accidental foulness, but the character and nature of the people to which he belonged. Like them, he was beyond help and hope.*

*The seraphs would surely want him thrown into the eternal furnace of hell to justly suffer God's torment. 'My eyes have seen the King, the LORD Almighty.' Although God is spirit, He had stooped to reveal Himself in this vision and Isaiah was doomed. Israel and all humanity could never hope to live with this Holy One of Israel. This LORD could not be manipulated by the empty farce of religious ceremony. No one could survive the unbearable weight of His judgment.*

*As Isaiah grovelled in anguished terror on the ground for what seemed like an age, one of the seraphs peeled off. Having flown to the altar of sacrifice and taken a burning coal, it flew towards him. Surely death and hell were upon him. But as the seraph touched the red-hot coal to his corrupted mouth, he spoke with unexpected words of tender assurance. 'Your guilt is taken away and your sin atoned for,' he said. Isaiah slowly lifted his eyes in relief and wonder. The sacrificial offerings of the altar from which the coal came had satisfied God's justice. His sin, dreadful though it was, had been pardoned, literally 'ransomed'. The cost and penalty of his sin had been paid by another. And to indicate the personal nature of this pardon, the coal was being touched directly to his lips, the place of his deepest awareness of sin. The words clarified what the action could not. He was no longer guilty before God. Isaiah had done nothing. This was wholly the initiative of God, a gift of His kindness.*

*Joy now flooded Isaiah's soul. He slumped in relief as he struggled to comprehend. How amazing was this God! How immense, not only in power but also in grace! How beautiful was His goodness! He had never dreamt that God was so glorious, so beautiful, so ... holy!*

*And then he realised that his own experience was the only hope for Israel. The holiness of God meant their condemnation unless they too were cleansed by a substitutionary sacrifice.*

But the vision wasn't finished. Isaiah now heard the voice of the Lord talking with Himself, as if He were plural: 'Whom shall I send? And who will go for us?' It was obvious that the Lord intended to send a preacher to proclaim this vision to Israel.

Isaiah was eager to respond. He felt ecstatic with the joy of forgiveness. How he longed for his family and nation to know this King – awesome in power, terrifying in judgment, yet so gracious in mercy. He was ready for anything. 'Here am I,' he cried, in the famous words of faithful Abraham, Samuel and David. 'Send me!' He could not go without God's commission. He could not presume to speak except with words from the LORD. But if God could use him, weak and wicked though he was, he would gladly preach this vision.

The Lord spoke again: 'Go and tell this people ...' He proceeded to give Isaiah a message of awful judgment. Isaiah must speak in the knowledge that, as he spoke, his hearers would be condemned to spiritual death, unable to understand what he was talking about. He was to be the instrument of the LORD's judgment until the cities and fields were laid waste by foreign armies! But God announced that out of this judgment upon the sin of His people, there would come hope, like a little branch from a great oak tree that has been felled to the ground. A 'holy seed', someone with the holy character of God, would come to rescue His people from the judgment they deserved. And Isaiah now knew from personal experience that the joy of pardon could only come after deep conviction of sin.

Isaiah rose to his feet a new man, the commissioned prophet of the Holy One of Israel. From now on, he would speak to the people of the holiness of God. He would preach on the holiness of His transcendent and righteous sovereignty, on the holiness of His just punishment of sin, and on the holiness of His gracious mercy in providing the sacrifice necessary to ransom sinners from hell. The holiness of God would be the theme of his life, preaching and writing, and he would be known as the prophet of holiness.

The apostolic gospel declares the coming of God in Jesus not only to be our incarnate King, sacrificial Saviour and resurrected Lord, but also our returning Judge (Romans 2 v 16). When we preach that Jesus is Lord, we not only proclaim that Jesus is risen to rule, but also that He will return to destroy. This is the 'eternal gospel' to proclaim to those who live on the earth: 'Fear God and give Him glory, because the hour of his judgment has come' (Revelation 14 v 6). This judgment will be like a terrible harvest in which the nations will be reaped by the Son of Man from their graves and tipped into the winepress of God's wrath and crushed in just judgement at the command of the Son of Man Himself, until their blood flows out like an ocean to the depth of a horse's bridle for 180 miles in all directions (Revelation 14). These are graphic images.

When we are asked what the message of the Bible is, we may reply in the famous words given by Karl Barth at a press conference at Princeton Seminary in 1961. At that time the world's most famous living theologian, Dr Barth was asked: 'What is the greatest theological statement ever made?'

After a long pause for thoughtful reflection, the great man replied: 'Jesus loves me, this I know, for the Bible tells me so.' True enough. But if you had asked the same question of Dr Martin Lloyd-Jones, the great preacher of Westminster Chapel, London, he would have replied with his often-repeated reference to the words of John the Baptist in Matthew 3 v 7: 'Flee the wrath to come!' Lloyd-Jones observed in 1930:

> Present-day religion far too often soothes the conscience instead of awakening it; and produces a sense of self-satisfaction and eternal safety rather than a sense of our unworthiness and the likelihood of eternal damnation.[2]

Indeed, if we are not preaching the wrath to come, we are not telling people the truth, nor giving them one of the best reasons for turning to Christ.

And if we don't tell people, who will? The devil won't tell people. His lie is published everywhere: 'You won't surely die' – hell is a medieval nightmare! The world won't tell people. It scoffs and asks, 'Where is this coming he promised ...? Everything goes on as it always has!' The false prophets in the church won't tell people either. They proclaim: 'Peace! Peace!' when there is no peace. Evangelistic courses that don't ever get to explaining judgement, heaven and hell, fall well short of explaining the biblical gospel (however popular they are). Without understanding that God is offended by our rebellion and should finally throw us out of His home for continually using and rejecting Him, we will never understand the love of Jesus shown at the cross. Christ's death is loving because He suffered the penalty for our sin. This is very simple and very powerful – the 'lost message of Jesus' is that God came to swap places with us because He loves us.

The problem is that no one wants to tell people bad news. Since Christianity is coming under increasing assault from a secular, permissive and pluralistic agenda, we shy away from warning of judgment with appropriate concern. But without hearing the bad news, the good news will never sound so fantastic. As Isaiah found, it was only when he realised how holy God is that he realised how sinful he was. And it was only when he realised how sinful he was that he realised how wonderful God's grace is. Preaching sin and judgment is the necessary preparation for preaching Christ and grace. It is no accident that the times of spiritual revival in the UK, such as in the Evangelical Revival of Whitefield and Wesley in the 18th century, or in South Wales in the early 20th century, were marked by preaching of judgment as well as of Christ.

The courage we will need to proclaim the message of judgment in our own day will only come from the same convictions that were granted to Isaiah in his famous vision described in Isaiah 6. This commissioning was foundational to the whole of his preaching and writing ministry, taken up with the holiness of God.

Chapters 1-5 reveal that Judah had become pluralistic and materialistic – like western culture today. If the nations were ever to come streaming to Zion in the kingdom of God, then the LORD would have to punish sin and rescue His people from their judgement. Isaiah was shown how this could happen. His personal experience illustrated the message he would have to proclaim concerning the holiness, judgment and forgiveness of God.

## He was given a fresh sense of God's holiness! (v 1-4)

This vision of the awesome holiness of God shows something of how He is today in His glory, even at this moment, for the song of the seraphs is still the chorus of the heavenly gathering (Revelation 4). We need to recover Isaiah's sense of the transcendent consuming righteousness of the LORD to whom we pray and in whose presence we live.

Moreover, this vision also demonstrates the holiness of Jesus. In John 12 v 40-41, John quotes from Isaiah 6 and says that Isaiah saw Jesus' glory. Of course, this was not the body of Jesus, for Jesus had not yet assumed a normal human body. But the person of Jesus, God the Son, being the eternal image of God, is the one whose presence was made manifest in this vision. God the Son accommodated Himself to human comprehension in this vision. He did so to motivate Isaiah and us to preach the gospel. This holy character of God is still Jesus' character. We must not domesticate and sanitise Jesus.

We need to recover this motivation to mission. In 2 Corinthians 5 v 11, the apostle Paul says: 'Since, then, we know what it is to fear the Lord, we try to persuade men.' A fresh sense of the holiness of God will help us to remember who it is who will examine our lives and will judge the sins of the unforgiven. As the great Welsh preacher Dr Martyn Lloyd-Jones once said in a sermon in Aberavon:

> I am not afraid of being charged as I frequently am, of trying to frighten you, for I am definitely trying to do so. If the wondrous love

of God in Christ Jesus and the hope of glory is not sufficient to attract you, then, such is the value I attach to the worth of your soul, I will do my utmost to alarm you with a sight of the terrors of hell.[3]

Humble willingness to preach the gospel begins with seeing how holy God is.

### He was given a fresh sense of judgment! (v 5)

Having seen the holiness of God, Isaiah was overwhelmed with guilt and awareness of his sin. He describes it here as uncleanness or moral corruption. God gives many perspectives upon the sinful condition of man. In Genesis 3 sin is described as rebellion against our Creator in disbelief, defiance and disobedience.

In Romans 1 sin is described as idolatry that redesigns God into the way we prefer Him to be. We will give our worship to other gods whom we prefer, or to versions of God that are more convenient, or to things and people other than God. Our favourite idol is our own image, which we worship with great devotion. In Ephesians 1, sin is seen as spiritual death in slavery. This slavery is a captivity or addiction to the ways of this world, the influence of Satan and the desires of our own flesh. It condemns us to condemnation and punishment from which we cannot escape. Rebellion, idolatry and slavery.

In Mark 7 Jesus says our hearts are filthy. He says: 'What comes out of a man is what makes him "unclean". For from within, out of men's hearts, come evil thoughts, sexual immorality, theft, murder, adultery, greed, malice, deceit, lewdness, envy, slander, arrogance and folly. All these evils come from inside and make a man "unclean"' (v 20-23). None of us can be guilty of all these corruptions, but many are all too familiar. It is this image of filthiness that overwhelmed Isaiah in his vision.

He now realised that he was a sinner in the hands of a righteously angry God. He cried out: 'I am ruined!' Not annihilated, but crushed and collapsed. The New Testament offers three horrific perspectives upon hell that Jesus often used. He said it was like punishment in the roasting fire of a furnace; like isolation in utter darkness; and like the destruction of consuming worms. These are, of course, just images. But Jesus thought them appropriate to convey the horror of life without God in the place where His justice is done. And these horrors are eternal.

A man appropriately called Fudge once tried to suggest that these images should be put in order, meaning that the unforgiven are first excluded, then punished, and then destroyed or annihilated. But the destruction of the Bible is ruination, not termination; and nowhere does the Bible suggest such an order. Rather, these images are three perspectives upon the same experience; Jesus explicitly says that as believers enter the life of the age to come, so unbelievers enter the punishment of the age to come (Matthew 25 v 46). If the life of God's people is everlasting, so is the punishment of His enemies. If hell is not everlasting for the unsaved, then heaven is not everlasting for the saved. These are sobering truths, but denying the horror of God's wrath helps nobody.

Isaiah was overcome with a proper sense of guilt and judgment before the holiness of God. Now he was ready to hear good news!

### He was given a fresh sense of forgiveness! (v 6)

Now he could be forgiven. The live coal from the altar symbolises the sacrifices made there, which, in turn, prefigure the sacrifice of Christ on the cross. There Jesus satisfied the Father for all our sin by suffering the penalty we deserve.

A leading Church of England cleric has recently publicly denied that Christ suffered our punishment, calling such a view 'repulsive' and 'insane', and one that makes God sound like a 'psychopath'. It's therefore worth remembering the words of Isaiah himself, familiar from Handel's Messiah, which are utterly clear about Christ's death:

> But he was pierced for our transgressions, he was crushed for our iniquities; the punishment that brought us peace was upon him, and

> by his wounds we are healed. We all, like sheep, have gone astray,
> each of us has turned to his own way; and the LORD has laid on him
> the iniquity of us all **Isaiah 53 v 5-6**

A good illustration of what Jesus did is provided in the wonderful heroism of Bill Deacon, the winchman of an air-sea rescue helicopter operating out of Bressay in the Shetland Islands, for which he was posthumously awarded the George Cross medal. In November 1997, the *Green Lily* cargo vessel was grounded on rocks and breaking up in mountainous waves. The lifeboats could no longer get to the stricken vessel to save the remaining crew on board.

Bill Deacon realised that the only hope of saving the men was to descend from the helicopter in the middle of the storm onto the deck of the ship. Once on the deck, he attached each of the remaining crew to his winch and, in his place, they were raised to safety. As the last man was rescued, Deacon was swept off the boat by the waves and his body was found a few days later further down the coast. He made the supreme sacrifice for those crew and no doubt today they would do anything to honour his memory.

In similar fashion, Christ descended into our world and, swapping places with us so that we could be raised to safety, gave His life in our place on the cross. Anyone who has been saved by Jesus will do anything to honour Him.

Aware that he had been forgiven by the provision of a sacrifice to cleanse his particular sins, Isaiah was now full of willingness to serve. When he overheard God talking with himself of who would go to His people, Isaiah offered to go. Given a message of judgment of sin, but also of hope beyond judgment, Isaiah was willing to preach. It is striking that Jesus took these same words upon His own lips as the commissioned prophet of God to the world, pronouncing God's judgment upon his hearers (Mark 4).

The big lesson for us is that Isaiah's motivation in preaching the gospel of judgment and hope derived from a series of fresh realisations. His willingness to preach the gospel came from his fresh sense of forgiveness; his sense of forgiveness came from his fresh sense of judgment; his sense of judgment came from his fresh sense of God's holiness.

The remedy for cold-heartedness in gospel ministry and evangelism is not more commands or guilt: it all starts with understanding how holy God is. Only then will God's judgment and then God's grace overwhelm us once more with willingness to serve. Perhaps in our evangelism training, and in our evangelism itself, we need to lift our eyes and the eyes of others to see the holiness of God. Everything follows from being humbled by him. 'Let us be thankful, and so worship God acceptably with reverence and awe, for our "God is a consuming fire"'(Hebrews 12 v 28-29).

For this humbling vision of the holiness of God, Isaiah belongs among 'a few good men'.

## BIBLE BACKGROUND

### *Isaiah*

Isaiah is an immense book, written in the eighth century before Christ, in which God is revealed as the 'Holy One' of Israel. The vision of chapter 6, central to the first section of the book (ch 1-12) is also foundational to the whole prophecy of Isaiah. Chapters 1-5 have revealed that, if the nations are to come to Israel to hear the word of the Lord from Jerusalem, Israel itself must be cleansed of its sin and renewed for service. The personal experience of Isaiah in chapter 6 reveals the only way of salvation for Israel. The nation must recognise the holiness of God, confess its sin, seek cleansing through God's substitutionary sacrifice and then be renewed for service. In the following chapters, 7-11, these themes are expanded further.

### *Isaiah's commissioning*

This process of facing God's holiness, confessing sin, receiving cleansing and offering to serve remains the path not only for Israel, but for all who wish to be saved today. Isaiah's commissioning reflects how all God's people are recruited to worship Him and become His prophets of the gospel of cleansing through Christ's sacrifice.

## Questions for group discussion

**1.** What was so overwhelming for Isaiah about this vision of God?

**2.** How sinful do we think we really are?

**3.** How guilty are we now before God?

**4.** Why was Isaiah suddenly so willing to preach the gospel?

### *References*
1 Robert Booth, Sunday Times (4.2.07).
2 *D. Martyn Lloyd-Jones, The First Forty Years* by Iain H. Murray, Banner of Truth Trust, 1982, p202.
3 Ibid, p216.

# DISTINCTIVE DANIEL

*'But Daniel resolved not to defile himself'*

DANIEL 1 v 8

The chameleon lizard is famous for being able to adapt its appearance. By changing its colour, it can quickly become camouflaged against all kinds of backgrounds so as to avoid predators. Chameleons are found mainly in Africa and some parts of Asia, though, given their special properties, perhaps it's hard to be certain!

Sometimes Christian men suffer from a kind of spiritual 'Chameleon Syndrome'. We adapt to whatever social background we are in so as to remain camouflaged and undetected by predators. It comes as a shock to friends and colleagues that we claim to be Christians at all. Often it is men who are popular and fearful of social ostracism who suffer from this 'Chameleon Syndrome' most severely. Intensely aware of peer pressure, desperate to belong in the world in which we move, Christians with 'Chameleon Syndrome' can remain undetected for years, camouflaged… like lizards.

The trouble is that this syndrome may be threatening our salvation. We cannot hide from being identified with Christ and still expect to be saved. Jesus said:

> If anyone is ashamed of me and my words in this adulterous and sinful generation, the Son of Man will be ashamed of him when he comes in his Father's glory with the holy angels. **Mark 8 v 38**

We cannot just adapt to secular culture. God says: 'So I tell you this, and insist on it in the Lord, that you must no longer live as the Gentiles do, in the futility of their thinking' (Ephesians 4 v 17). We cannot worship without being different from the world around us. We read in Scripture: 'Offer your bodies as living sacrifices, holy and pleasing to God – this is your reasonable act of worship. Do not conform any longer to the pattern of this world, but be transformed by the renewing of your mind' (Romans 12 v 1-2). Being a Christian means being distinctive.

The book of Daniel is for Christians beginning to suffer from Chameleon Syndrome. It challenges us to be distinctive like Daniel. The central message of the whole book comes in 1 v 8.

> In the third year of the reign of Jehoiakim king of Judah, Nebuchadnezzar king of Babylon came to Jerusalem and besieged it. And the Lord delivered Jehoiakim king of Judah into his hand, along with some of the articles from the temple of God. These he carried off to the temple of his god in Babylonia and put in the treasure-house of his god.

> Then the king ordered Ashpenaz, chief of his court officials, to bring in some of the Israelites from the royal family and the nobility – young men without any physical defect, handsome, showing aptitude for every kind of learning, well informed, quick to understand, and qualified to serve in the king's palace. He was to teach them the language and literature of the Babylonians. The king assigned them a daily amount of food and wine from the king's table. They were to be trained for three years, and after that they were to enter the king's service.

> Among these were some from Judah: Daniel, Hananiah, Mishael and Azariah. The chief official gave them new names: to Daniel, the name Belteshazzar; to Hananiah, Shadrach; to Mishael, Meshach; and to Azariah, Abednego.

> *But Daniel resolved not to defile himself with the royal food and wine, and he asked the chief official for permission not to defile himself in this way.* Now God had caused the official to show favour and sympathy to Daniel, but the official told Daniel, 'I am afraid of my lord the king, who has assigned your food and drink. Why should he see you looking worse than the other young men of your age? The king would then have my head because of you.'

Daniel then said to the guard whom the chief official had appointed over Daniel, Hananiah, Mishael and Azariah, 'Please test your servants for ten days: Give us nothing but vegetables to eat and water to drink. Then compare our appearance with that of the young men who eat the royal food, and treat your servants in accordance with what you see.' So he agreed to this and tested them for ten days.

At the end of the ten days they looked healthier and better nourished than any of the young men who ate the royal food. So the guard took away their choice food and the wine they were to drink and gave them vegetables instead.

To these four young men God gave knowledge and understanding of all kinds of literature and learning. And Daniel could understand visions and dreams of all kinds.

At the end of the time set by the king to bring them in, the chief official presented them to Nebuchadnezzar. The king talked with them, and he found none equal to Daniel, Hananiah, Mishael and Azariah; so they entered the king's service. In every matter of wisdom and understanding about which the king questioned them, he found them ten times better than all the magicians and enchanters in his whole kingdom.

And Daniel remained there until the first year of King Cyrus.

**Daniel 1**

*The four young Hebrew lads stared, hearts pounding, at the sealed scrolls placed on the table in front of them. All the other academy students, the elite from various nations conquered by the Babylonians, had already opened their scrolls to discover their grades. All eyes were now turned upon these young men who'd made their notorious public stand for the LORD, the God of Israel. Everyone was talking about them. How would they fare? Life was cheap at Nebuchadnezzar's court, and having challenged the system, they knew their lives were at stake.*

*At the far end of the royal banqueting hall, on the raised platform, flanked by an army of attendants, advisers and Imperial*

Guards, was Nebuchadnezzar's table. There the royal household and government dignitaries were eating in opulent splendour, entertained by musicians and poets. In front of the king were rows of tables, laden with sumptuous food, at which lesser officials and humiliated foreign rulers ate quietly, contemplating their total subservience to the all-conquering Babylonian emperor. At the lower end of the hall were the academy students. As Daniel looked up anxiously towards the royal table, he caught King Nebuchadnezzar staring at him with a look of intrigued fascination. Daniel, Hananiah, Mishael and Azariah, the finest young princes of Israel ever brought to the academy, stared nervously at the scrolls which now determined their fate.

Daniel recalled how he and the other Israelite princes had been brought to Babylon three years earlier in 605 BC. Jehoiakim, the wicked king of Judah, had stupidly switched his allegiance back to Egypt in rebellion against the Babylonian Empire. Retribution was swift. The armies of Nebuchadnezzar, then prince and now king of Babylon, had swiftly besieged and crushed Jerusalem. Rather than being executed like those in high office, Daniel and others of young Israelite nobility had been brought to the academy for training in the culture of Babylon. Clearly, this was intended to educate the next generation of Judean leaders in Babylonian ways, to ensure the quiet submission of Israel. Daniel and his friends were under immense pressure to conform meekly, as all the other students had done.

It certainly looked as if the faith and culture of Israel were now finished. Having previously been subject to attacks from Egypt and Assyria, Jerusalem, supposed to be the dwelling-place of the LORD, had been easily overwhelmed by the pagan Babylonian armies. The great temple of Solomon had been desecrated and ransacked by the worshippers of Chaldean gods like Anu (the heaven-god), Marduk (the air-god) and Ea (god of deep waters). Its holy furnishings and articles were shipped off to Babylon as spoils for the shrine of Marduk (or Bel). The royal line of Judean kings appointed by the LORD, tracing back 400 years to Saul, David and Solomon, had ended in puppet rulers subject to Babylon. To all appearances, the LORD, the God of Israel, was utterly defeated: a myth that had died with an ancient culture.

And Babylon was very impressive to the minds of these young men. It was the splendid and sophisticated capital of the most powerful civilisation the world had ever known. After a long journey that emphasised their distance from the past, the young Jewish boys were overcome by the sheer scale and grandeur of Babylon, strategically placed by the great river Euphrates. The 27 kilometres of double outer walls were so enormous that chariots were driving along them.

As they'd entered the magnificent Ishtar gates, travelling down the glorious Procession Way towards the Temple of Marduk, they'd seen the famous tower of Babel, symbolic of human pride and achievement. Soon they saw the amazing hanging gardens built for the queen, tumbling down from the palace towards the river. Then the numerous temples and splendid palaces of the city rebuilt by Nebuchadnezzar. This certainly looked like the pluralistic culture of the future. This city, which embodied human self-aggrandisement in hostile rebellion against God, made Jerusalem, which they'd been told was 'the perfection of beauty, the joy of the whole world', seem rather pathetic.

As they'd been personally welcomed to the Palace Academy by Prime Minister Ashpenaz, it was obvious that this was a golden opportunity for Daniel and his friends. All the students enrolled for the three-year courses were physically fit, highly intelligent, well-educated and privileged teenagers from the ruling classes of nations all over the world. These were the finest intellects and most talented athletes in the empire, being trained in the language, literature and culture of Babylon by the best Chaldean professors at Ashurbanipal's famous library. They had launched into fascinating studies in mathematics, natural sciences, medicine and engineering, for which their own backgrounds in the wisdom and science of Solomon had well prepared them. And there were new, faith-related studies, too. Astrology, divination, exorcism and all kinds of magic arts were important classes and each day began with prayers to gods they'd previously been forbidden even to mention.

They were treated very well, living in the palace quarters and dining in the king's own banqueting hall. These were heady privileges for young lads so far from Judah and with no hope of ever going home. And there were great prospects, as they were repeatedly reminded. Graduates could expect to serve in the government. And the best way to help their families and homelands was to fit in, gain what promotion they could, and hope to acquire some influence over conditions back home. Conversely, protest was pointless. Countless other young men would jump at this chance to avoid the harsh conditions of slave labour at the Imperial building sites.

As if to erase all memory of the LORD they once served, their names as well as their clothes were changed into the Babylonian tradition. Daniel (God is my Judge), Hananiah (God has been gracious), Mishael (None is like God) and Azariah (God has helped) were now to have the names of Babylonian gods included in their own: Belteshazzar, Shadrach, Meshach and Abednego. They now looked, sounded and felt like good Babylonians. But Daniel knew that all was not what it seemed.

Daniel knew that, far from being defeated, the LORD, the God of Israel, was actually arranging everything that was happening. Only months before Jehoiakim had rebelled against Babylon, everyone in Judah knew that the brave prophet Jeremiah had warned of punishment for the king and all Israel because Jehoiakim had persistently refused to listen to the words of the LORD's prophet commanding him and the nation to stop worshipping other gods. Jeremiah had foretold the arrival and victory of Nebuchadnezzar, the destruction of Jerusalem and ruin of Israel, *and the exile of many from Judah for 70 years. But Jehoiakim hadn't listened.*

*Daniel knew that the LORD Himself had delivered Jehoiakim and Jerusalem into Nebuchadnezzar's hands. The destruction of Jerusalem had, in fact, made Daniel fear the LORD more than the Babylonian king. And Daniel realised that he and his friends weren't popular and successful at the academy by accident. The special favour shown them by Ashpenaz and the other officials was being engineered by God for a purpose. They knew the Scriptures about Joseph in the court of the Egyptian Pharaoh. Every Jewish boy was raised on the stories of how the LORD had blessed his moral faithfulness with promotion to become prime minister of Egypt at the time of the great famine. Daniel knew that, particularly because of their standing in Israelite society at this time, they too must make their stand. He'd discussed it with the other three and they'd prayed furiously about it. They were understandably frightened, but were with him. A line must be drawn in the sand.*

*'Daniel resolved not to defile himself.' He'd asked the official to be excused the king's provision of meat and wine and for the four Hebrew lads to be fed only with vegetables. It was nothing to do with the food. Of course, it was always offered to Babylonian idols, but so were the vegetables (and Daniel had heard of Isaiah's famous declarations that these Babylonian gods didn't even exist). It wasn't to do with kosher preparation, because they were refusing the wine as well. It wasn't to do with wanting a simpler peasant lifestyle or being ascetic. It was just that Daniel wanted to stop the assimilation, stop the compromising, stop the adaptation, stop the public assumption that they were becoming Babylonian. He just had to be distinctive! Other people could choose another way to be distinctive if they wanted. But he knew it was vital for their souls that they make a stand – to align them-selves publicly with the LORD, the God of Israel, before they total-*

*ly capitulated. It was a matter of spiritual allegiance, not ceremonial scruple; a matter of defilement, not diet.*

*Of course, the outcome was well known. The official had been terrified of irritating the king. But the guard had agreed to test the lads with a diet of vegetables. Ten days later, they were healthier and fitter than everyone else. And God had greatly blessed them with what they needed at the academy. As they'd set themselves to study, the LORD had granted them knowledge and understanding of all kinds of literature and sciences. Daniel could even understand the meaning of visions and dreams, and the Chaldean scholars were seriously impressed. But now their final examinations had arrived. They'd each been thoroughly assessed by the king himself. He was, himself, a formidable intellect who insisted on interviewing the final-year students personally. Daniel was expected to top the year, with the other three not far behind. But the stakes were high. The rumours were that Nebuchadnezzar was none too pleased at their challenging the educational curriculum. Some of the priests were muttering about spiritual afflictions from the gods. All would be revealed in the scrolls.*

*The banqueting hall hushed as the king's attention was focused upon these Hebrew lads as they opened their scrolls. Daniel stared at his grades. He hardly dared believe his eyes. First class honours, the Ashurbanipal prize for top of class, and a special award from Nebuchadnezzar for attaining the highest grade in all subjects.*

*Overwhelmed with relief, eyes bright with excitement, Daniel looked up to find his friends equally ecstatic. They'd all passed with flying colours. They together bowed their heads to utter a quiet prayer of thanksgiving. When they looked up towards the high table, Nebuchadnezzar was looking approvingly in their direction. He raised his glass to these bright stars of the future. Daniel smiled in his soul. The Most High was still sovereign, even in this pagan land. They had been right to resolve not to defile themselves. Right to be... distinctive!*

Though Daniel lived 2,600 years ago, his situation is very familiar to Christian men living in the UK today.

## Like Daniel, we are under pressure to conform

The Christian faith seems to be in terminal decline. Church leaders and bishops are ignored, ridiculed and disgraced. Church buildings are turned into restaurants and fashionable flats, and the old pews sold for wealthy homes. Young men are being educated in the culture of pagan pluralism. Three years at a top university will usually present able young Christians with overwhelming pressures to compromise, adapt and eventually become assimilated into godless materialism and agnostic pluralism. Overwhelmed by impressive educational establishments (which hide their Christian origins), lured by the prospect of glittering future careers and blind to the suppression of philosophical presumptions in their lectures and reading lists, they can easily be moulded to become 'good Babylonians.'

And such pressures are not felt just by students. The pressures to conform are just as oppressive in an office, hospital ward and classroom.

## Like Daniel, we must resolve not to defile ourselves

Although I have never tried it, I am told that if you heat the water slowly enough, frogs will allow themselves to be cooked, boiled to death, without complaint, because they don't recognise the change that is slowly going on.

There are many Christians who are being spiritually boiled to death because they don't realise how morally compromised they are becoming. In such situations, Christians under pressure need to know that the LORD, Jesus, the Most High, is sovereign over the kingdoms of men, however powerful and pagan they may be.

Like Daniel, we must 'resolve not to defile ourselves'. We need to draw a line in the sand where we say: 'Stop! I will not adapt and compromise any further.' Where exactly we draw that line will vary from person to person and situation to situation. We must all obey the law of Christ, but where we decide to draw a line in those matters which are not proscribed in God's law must be a matter of prayerful decision, respected by other Christians. Here are three examples:

- I know of a Christian rugby player who found that he was repeatedly dishonouring Christ after rugby matches simply because he was drinking too much. So he 'resolved not to defile himself' any more and gave up drink entirely. Being an enormous lock forward at a club where most players got absolutely smashed after games, this was quite unusual. It made him distinctive and led to many opportunities to explain the gospel to his teammates. The Bible forbids drunkenness but not all alcohol, so it won't be necessary for everyone to give up drinking alcohol. But since so much immorality and failure among Christians is directly related to drinking too much, it must be worth considering. After all, the apostle Paul warned:

> Among you there must not be even a hint of sexual immorality, or of any kind of impurity, or of greed, because these are improper for God's holy people. Nor should there be obscenity, foolish talk or coarse joking, which are out of place, but rather thanksgiving. For of this you can be sure: No immoral, impure or greedy person – such a man is an idolater – has any inheritance in the kingdom of Christ and of God. **Ephesians 5 v 3-5**

- I know of a Christian family who 'resolved not to defile themselves' by getting rid of their television. They simply put it away in the loft because they recognised that they were being boiled alive in the ungodly culture promoted by it. They keep up with the world through radio and newspapers, and report that, although the kids complained at first, the whole family is now contentedly a lot more Christian at home. They are now distinctively Christian. It may not be wise for everyone, but it's worth considering!

- I know of churches that have decided to declare themselves in 'temporarily impaired communion' (ie: no longer friends) with their bishop because he will not publicly condemn sexual activity outside of marriage. They feel they must publicly distance themselves from immorality if they are not to become assimilated within structures that are denying the teaching of Scripture. Not everyone will want to do this, but as a matter of conscience these churches feel they must draw a line somewhere. If this is not what our church does, it's worth considering what we will do to ensure that we are distinctively Christian.

## Like Daniel, we can expect to be blessed in the coming kingdom of God

Daniel was not really a brave young man, but a wise young man. He wasn't fooled by the prestige and power of Babylon. He knew that the Most High rules over all the kingdoms of men. Human kingdoms come and go, as the poet Shelley memorably expressed it in Ozymandias, a poem about a long-forgotten eastern potentate. It tells of a traveller who had discovered a broken statue in the middle of a desert, all that remained of what was once a great dynasty and civilisation:

> And on the pedestal these words appear:
> 'My name is Ozymandias, king of kings:
> Look on my works, ye mighty, and despair!'
> Nothing beside remains: round the decay
> Of that colossal wreck, boundless and bare,
> The lone and level sands stretch far away.1

From glory to dust. How true it is that the great and powerful, the wealthy and the famous of today, are forgotten the day after tomorrow. But one day, the everlasting kingdom of God will come with the Son of Man. All human power will be destroyed and those who have resolved not to defile themselves – those who are distinctive like Daniel – will rise to shine like stars in heaven.

In Daniel's case, the LORD chose to bless him with success and promotion in life. There is no promise that God's blessings are guaranteed this side of death – after all, the most distinctive man of all was crucified for His resolution to remain undefiled! But Daniel's experience shows that God can reward in this life if He wants too. In Daniel's case, this first test of his resolution was critical for preparing him for bigger tests to come (such as his faithfulness to the LORD in prayer when he later got thrown to the lions). It may be that faithfulness in resolving to be undefiled in small matters today will prepare and qualify us for greater tests to come.

Daniel certainly does demonstrate that the LORD sees our resolutions to be distinctive for Him and that He will honour us for it in His good time. It would be wonderful if, after we had died, people were able to say of each of us: 'He resolved not to defile himself – he resolved to be distinctive!' Daniel challenges each of us to consider where we are becoming compromised and what we must resolve to do, or not to do, in order to remain distinctive. Daniel belongs among 'a few good men' because he was distinctive.

## BIBLE BACKGROUND

### *The Bible*

The New Testament tells us what the Bible is written about, who it was written by and what it was written for (2 Timothy 3 v 15-17):

- All Scripture (including the Old Testament) is about salvation through faith in Christ.
- All Scripture was written by authors who crafted exactly what God was 'breathing out' by his Holy Spirit through them.
- 'All Scripture is for teaching, rebuking, correcting and training in righteousness so that the man of God [primarily the Bible teacher but including all believers] may be thoroughly equipped for every good work.'
- All the equipment we will need from the Spirit of God for living the Christian life is in the Bible.

Therefore, the Old Testament book of Daniel, (written in the 6th century BC) is also about faith in Christ, written by the living God for our godliness. When we read Daniel, it talks about God's people living in exile in a pagan country, far from the kingdom of God. It was to help Christians today serve the Most High as we too live in pagan cultures far from the kingdom of God.

## *Daniel*

The structure of Daniel reveals its principal themes.

Ch 1 Daniel resolves not to defile himself (the book's recommended wisdom)
Ch 2 Daniel interprets the king's dream (a statue smashed by a divine rock)
Ch 3 Daniel's friends refuse to worship an idol (fiery furnace)
Ch 4 Nebuchadnezzar humbled like a donkey (the Most High is sovereign)
Ch 5 Belshazzar's feast interrupted by 'finger' writing on wall (judgment)
Ch 6 Daniel refusing to pray to Darius (lions' den)
Ch 7 Daniel's dream of four beasts (and a 'Son of Man' given all power)
Ch 8 Daniel's dream about a sheep and goat (persecution to come)
Ch 9 Daniel's prayer of confession (and the promise of a desolating sacrilege)
Ch 10 Daniel's vision of a man in linen (directing the history of nations)
Ch 11 Revelations of future battles (and the 'anti-Christ' exalting himself)
Ch 12 Reassurance that Daniel will rest in death and rise to an inheritance

Chapter 1 gives the aim of the book – that God's people should follow Daniel's example and resolve not to defile themselves as they serve God in the pagan cultures where they live.

This resolution (1 v 8) is then reinforced by chapters 2-7, which are proclaimed to the whole world in Aramaic. The heart of the section is chapters 4-5 with the four-times repeated phrase: 'The Most High is sovereign over the kingdoms of men and gives them to anyone he wishes'. (God is sovereign over the nations or Jesus Christ is Lord – the 'gospel'). Chapters 3 and 6 are parallel accounts of faithful believers refusing to worship anyone but God and being thrown to their deaths (Shadrach, Meshach and Abednego into the fiery furnace and Daniel into the lions' den). In both cases, God demonstrates His sovereign power to save His people, and the respective emperors send decrees throughout the Babylonian Empire that all must worship God. God is sovereign to save! Chapters 2 and 7 contain parallel visions of four human kingdoms (identified as Babylon, Medo-Persia, Greece and Rome) being replaced by God's kingdom, represented by a divine rock, and the Son of Man, the coming kingdom of God under Christ. God is sovereign over the future.

Chapters 8 to 12 then reveal that, before God's kingdom comes, God's people must suffer terrible persecution under evil human tyrants.

The message of the book is: resolve not to defile yourself (ch 1), because the Most High is sovereign over the kingdoms of men (ch 4-5) to rescue His people (ch 3, 6) and over the future (ch 2, 7), though we must suffer persecution before the kingdom of Christ finally comes. In summary, serve God in a pagan land because the Most High is sovereign over the kingdoms of men – be distinctive!

## Questions for group discussion

1. What are the pressures upon us to conform to the world around us?

2. How should Christians today be distinctive?

3. What should we resolve to do in order to remain distinctively Christian?

### *References*

1 Percy Bysshe Shelley, in *A Treasury of the World's Best Loved Poems*, Avenel Books, Crown publishers, 1961, p76.

# 8 PASTORAL PAUL

*'I am innocent of the blood of all men'*

ACTS 20 v 26

'Pastoral Ministry' is a confusing term. To many people it seems to mean a kind of Christian therapy. Sometimes a church leader is described as being a great Bible-teacher but a hopeless 'pastor', meaning they lack people skills. Someone is said to have a 'pastoral' heart because they have a love for people. A church decides to develop its 'pastoral ministries', meaning it wants to invest in ministries of personal care and compassion.

Certainly, the Bible expects church leaders to be kind to everyone. All believers are urged to love other people. Churches are expected to develop ministries of personal compassion. But these are aspects of loving care expected of *all* Christians, and, surprisingly, are *not* what the Bible describes as the 'pastoral' or 'shepherding' ministry expected of church leaders. Of course, church leaders must be mature Christians, setting an example of Christ-like kindness, practical love and personal compassion. But this is their 'personal ministry' rather than their 'pastoral ministry'.

So what is 'pastoral' ministry? We need to know because, although only some of us will be appointed as pastors, all of us will want to encourage and pray for our church pastors to provide the ministry that God knows we need from them. And those of us who exercise leadership in the local church, and may be responsible for selecting a new pastor, will need to be clear about what ministry is, if we are to ensure that our church does not become deflected into important, but secondary activities.

To understand what 'pastoral ministry' is we must begin with God, who repeatedly describes himself as the 'Shepherd', or Pastor, of his people. In the Bible, God's pastoral ministry is *always* about saving or 'redeeming' His people. So, He describes His rescue of Israel from slavery in Egypt in 'pastoral' terms: 'He brought His people out like a flock; He led them like sheep through the desert.' (Psalm 78 v 52). Likewise, in Psalm 23, David describes God as his Shepherd leading him through life and death.

God's 'pastoral ministry' then, is redeeming people from the kingdom of darkness into the kingdom of his Son.

The Old Testament records that God appointed prophets, priests and kings to this 'pastoral ministry' in Israel. But they repeatedly failed him on two counts. First, they were selfish rather than serving. Secondly, they proclaimed the delusions of their own minds rather than the word of God. God pronounced His judgment upon those shepherds (let modern pastors beware) but He never abandoned His flock. He promised He would come to '… gather them and … watch over his flock like a shepherd.' (Jer 31 v 10).

As promised, God arrived in Jesus to be our 'Good Shepherd'. He served the sheep rather than Himself:

'I am the good shepherd; I know my sheep and my sheep know me … I lay down my life for the sheep. I have other sheep … I must bring them also. They too will listen to my voice, and there shall be one flock and one shepherd' **John 10 v 14-16**

People in Jesus' 'flock' are known by Him, saved by Him and united by him.

Moreover, the 'Good Shepherd' taught the word of God rather than the delusions of His own mind:

When Jesus landed and saw a large crowd, he had compassion on them, because they were like sheep without a shepherd. So he began teaching them many things. **Mark 6 v 34**

Jesus is the compassionate and guiding Pastor that everyone needs.

But while He is away in heaven, the risen Jesus has entrusted His flock to earthly 'pastors and teachers', through whom He continues to pastor His flock. The primary aim of 'pastoral ministry' today is to bring people to the Good Shepherd for *His* saving pastoral care.

Pastors today are like sheepdogs! The sheepdog's task is to round up the scattered sheep and herd them into a pen for the shepherd. The sheepdogs don't gather the sheep for themselves but only for the shepherd. The role of pastors is to gather the lost sheep to the Good Shepherd for His protection and guidance week by week.

*But how is this to be done?*

Nowhere is this kind of pastoral ministry more clearly explained than in the training given by the apostle Paul to the leaders of the Ephesian church whom he commanded: 'Be shepherds of the church of God'.

From Miletus, Paul sent to Ephesus for the elders of the church. When they arrived, he said to them: 'You know how I lived the whole time I was with you, from the first day I came into the province of Asia. I served the Lord with great humility and with tears, although I was severely tested by the plots of the Jews. You know that I have not hesitated to preach anything that would be helpful to you but have taught you publicly and from house to house. I have declared to both Jews and Greeks that they must turn to God in repentance and have faith in our Lord Jesus.

'And now, compelled by the Spirit, I am going to Jerusalem, not knowing what will happen to me there. I only know that in every city the Holy Spirit warns me that prison and hardships are facing me. However, I consider my life worth nothing to me, if only I may finish the race and complete the task the Lord Jesus has given me – the task of testifying to the gospel of God's grace.

'Now I know that none of you among whom I have gone about preaching the kingdom will ever see me again. Therefore, I declare to you today that I am innocent of the blood of all men. For I have not hesitated to proclaim to you the whole will of God. Keep watch over yourselves and all the flock of which the Holy Spirit has made you overseers. Be shepherds of the church of God, which he bought with his own blood. I know that after I leave, savage wolves will come in among you and will not spare the flock. Even from your own number men will arise and distort the truth in order to draw away disciples after them. So be on your guard! Remember that for three years I never stopped warning each of you night and day with tears.

'Now I commit you to God and to the word of his grace, which can build you up and give you an inheritance among all those who are sanctified. I have not coveted anyone's silver or gold or clothing. You yourselves know that these hands of mine have supplied my own needs and the needs of my companions. In everything I did, I showed you that by this kind of hard work we must help the weak, remembering the words the Lord Jesus himself said: "It is more blessed to give than to receive."'

When he had said this, he knelt down with all of them and prayed. They all wept as they embraced him and kissed him. What grieved them most was his statement that they would never see his face again. Then they accompanied him to the ship. **Acts 20 v 17-38**

*It was an emotional farewell at Miletus harbour that day. The elders who pastored the Ephesian churches now realised that they'd never see their beloved apostle again.*

*They owed so much to Paul. Most had come to Christ through his amazing Tyrannus Hall lectures during the wild two-and-a-half years he spent in Ephesus. They'd been raised in superstition, worshipping at the great temple of Artemis, but now they were leaders of a Christian church that was helping to plant churches all over the Galatian province. Christ had turned their lives upside down through the apostle. And now he was leaving, forever.*

*The freight-ship captain was anxious to be free of the coast by night-fall, so parting words were hurried. Paul's travelling companions were a motley crew. There were the Greeks entrusted with the 'Fellowship Gift'* for Jerusalem. Sopater was the muscle from Berea; the money was sure to be safe with this ex-legionary with the 'don't mess with me' face. The ever-dignified Aristarchus and Secundus from Thessalonica were the church emissaries. There was Gaius from nearby Derbe, Timothy (tipped to be their next senior pastor), Tychicus (Paul's ministry apprentice) and their own local boy Trophimus, leaving a promising engineering career for mission training.

And, of course, Dr Luke was there, constantly writing notes for his two-volume history of Jesus that probably no one would ever read...

They'd arrived early that morning on mules and carts after the fifty-kilometre trip from Ephesus, having stayed overnight in hostels. They'd been sworn to secrecy because Paul was anxious to get to Jerusalem with the gift for the Judean churches. He couldn't afford to be delayed either by the hospitality of old friends or the hostility of the Ephesian police.

But these elders desperately needed more training. None had been a Christian for very long. Paul wanted to head west for Rome and Spain and would probably never return. But he had to be sure they grasped the fundamentals of pastoral ministry. He was worried about the ambitions of some and about the materialism of the church. So he'd summoned them down to the Miletus Taverna for another of his legendary 'Pastoral Ministry Boot Camps'.

So after a modest breakfast (standard olive salad, fish and eggs), they'd arranged the benches around the apostle in the rooftop verandah they'd hired for the day. The sea breeze would keep them cool, while they talked, planned and prayed together.

They were all elders, the team of senior men appointed by Paul to pastor the church. Paul appointed such councils for every church he planted. He sometimes called them 'bishops', charged with overseeing the congregation. Paul often said that the health of the Ephesian church lay more in the loyalty to the gospel of these local leaders and their families than in the professional 'prophets' and 'teachers' who tended to come and go.

Paul began the day reminding them of his own ministry as a pattern for them: 'You know how I lived the whole time I was with you.'

They certainly knew him well. He'd made a massive effort to get involved in their lives and families, discussing the faith with their kids, praying at the dinner table, debating the biblical perspective on current social issues or church priorities. They found him no ascetic but a warm and caring man, tender as a nursing mother but as challenging as the best of fathers. He explained that sharing his life with the church like this protected him from 'patterns of professional pretence' and was good for them in modelling the application of his teaching, even though it revealed his weaknesses. He'd also developed his 'apprenticeship scheme' for young leaders, involving them in his ministry and taking them on his missionary journeys, because pastoral ministry is 'caught' as much as 'taught'.

'I served the Lord with great humility and with tears,' he said, 'although I was severely tested by the plots of the Jews.' Paul saw himself as working, not so much for the church, but as a slave for Christ. He'd sometimes graciously refused the requests of the church council to ignore Jesus' more controversial teaching in order not to offend Ephesian culture.

His talks on 'You can't serve two Gods' and 'Why homosexual practice is depraved' had caused uproar. He was especially hated by his own Jewish countrymen for preaching that Christ had to be crucified for Jews as much as for Gentiles. They'd responded with shocking political tactics to discredit and malign him. But it was the envious disloyalty of other Christian leaders that most often brought him to tears. Clearly these young Ephesians pastors must expect to face unpopularity and hostility like Paul, and Jesus before him.

He spent the whole morning explaining his pastoral ministry under the heading, 'Teach the Gospel', after which, their hearts burning within them, they broke for lunch. Some of the younger men went swimming. One or two lay down for a brief siesta. Paul's companions went to the village to buy fruit for the journey, but Paul walked with the two senior elders discussing a strategy for evangelism, church-planting and recruiting, training and deploying the next generation of gospel workers.

After lunch they gathered again for Paul's more specific reflections upon *the Ephesian churches. He urged them to 'Protect the church' and then to 'Give the Word'. And then it was time to leave.*

*When Paul knelt with them all to pray, these dignified leaders wept openly. Those who say that a Bible-teaching pastoral ministry is just about ideas have clearly never experienced it. Paul had brought God's Word deep into the hearts of these men and their families, rearranging their marriages, finances, parenting and plans. They now understood that Paul's pattern of pastoral ministry must be continued by them in Ephesus, because it was Jesus' pattern of pastoral ministry.*

*When it was time to cast off, there were the usual chaotic scenes – stupid jokes and brave words as they ushered Paul up the gang plank. When the boat finally slipped out of hearing into the gathering gloom, the shore party fell quiet. Someone suggested a short time of prayer back at the taverna before the journey back to Ephesus. With hearts heavy and heads spinning, they thanked God for Paul's time among them. They pleaded with God for power to take the task up themselves and to train others after them. Then the senior Elders solemnly announced that Timothy was to be employed as their new salaried 'Pastor' to lead the team. Everyone now understood what they meant.*

---

There are many competing models of 'pastoral ministry'. There is the priestly-ecclesiastical version with the 'men in black' celebrating Holy Communion at every opportunity. There is the business-executive version with the 'men in suits' organising conferences for everyone to attend. There is the therapeutic-counsellor version with the 'men in sandals' willing to listen to anyone for hours. And there is the social-activist version with the 'men in jeans' zealous to change the world.

What was the pastoral ministry commended by Paul to the elders at Miletus? It was essentially a Gospel-teaching ministry. He later wrote to them:

> The gifts he gave were that some would be pastors and teachers, to prepare God's people for works of service, so that the body of Christ may be built up until we all reach unity in the faith and in the knowledge of the Son of God and become mature, attaining to the whole measure of the fullness of Christ' **Ephesians 4 v 11**

Many people assume that a congregation is like a football crowd gathering to watch and cheer expensive stars demonstrating their skills on the pitch – so God's people gather to hear and applaud preachers showing off their skills for the entertainment of the church. In fact *it is the congregation* who are like the players on the field, witnessing to Christ before a watching world. The pastors are more like the slightly boring coaches who work behind the scenes to prepare the team to play. True pastoral ministry is Bible-teaching that brings a congregation to salvation and equips them for service.

## Teach the Gospel (20-27)

There were four major themes to Paul's teaching:

### 1. Teach repentance and faith in our Lord Jesus!

**Read v 20-21.** Paul taught God's gospel concerning 'our Lord Jesus' (v 21). The good news that saves is not *our story* or the story of our church or the story of the world or even the story of God the Father and his Holy Spirit. All these truths are important background to the gospel, but the *only* message that saves is about 'our Lord Jesus'.

Paul wrote that the gospel of God announces that Jesus is Christ our Lord: **Jesus** (the crucified preacher from Nazareth) **is the Christ** (the promised Saviour and King) **our Lord** (the risen and divine ruler and judge of all men) (Rom 1). He taught that Jesus Christ's lordship is expressed in His coming as King, His death for our sins and resurrection from the dead according to the scriptures, and His return to judge (1 Cor 15 v 1-7; Rom 2 v 16).

Paul persuaded his hearers that they needed to believe these gospel facts about Jesus in order to be saved. But he also insisted they must make *a personal commitment* to Christ Himself of whom these statements are true.

Controversially, Paul said that Jews and Greeks alike needed to repent and trust in Jesus – which incensed the Jews who regarded themselves as already saved by being the covenant people of Israel who observe the law. Repentance from sin means changing our minds to the depth of our wills – not merely hearing or agreeing with the gospel facts. It means being willing to change direction, and turning from sin to live under the rule of the Lord Jesus. The need for such repentance is tragically neglected in many current evangelistic materials and gospel presentations.

The other side of this turning from sin to God also involves 'faith', trusting and relying on Christ for salvation instead of ourselves. Although we are saved from the first moment we decisively repent and believe, the whole of the Christian life is marked by a continual repentance and faith. We are not *becoming* Christians over and over again, but bringing different areas of our lives under the loving rule of our saviour.

Paul didn't teach such gospel truths as dry intellectual doctrines unrelated to the personal needs and lives of his hearers. The gospel doctrines described in this passage have enormous relevance to our everyday lives. The common cause of much personal misery is quite simply *sin*. And the remedy for the selfishness, pride, violence, envy, lust, dishonesty and anger that ruin the lives and relationships of so many is often simple but deep repentance from sin, and simple trust in the forgiveness and power of 'our Lord Jesus'.

### 2. Teach the gospel of God's Grace!

**Read 22-24.** Paul was clearly not living for the approval of his family or colleagues, or an obituary in a Christian newspaper, but for Jesus. His life would be 'worth nothing' If he failed the Lord. Elders today must likewise care less for the approval of others and more for the approval of Christ.

The task given to the Apostle and passed on to pastors down the generations like a baton in a relay race, was 'testifying to the gospel of God's grace'. The Apostle suspected that some of the elders were eager to become 'teachers of the law' rather than teachers of grace (1 Tim 1); sadly, pastors sometimes indulge a similar appetite today. So he urged hem to teach God's 'grace'.

God's grace is His undeserved kindness and generosity toward us in Christ. Pastors will need to teach the great doctrines of grace outlined in the New Testament: **God's loving predestination** (we were chosen for holiness and adoption as sons); **God's providence** (provision of all that we need every day) and **God's preservation** (keeping us going to the end).

Especially, pastors must help us to cling tenaciously to the simple 'swap' at the heart of the gospel of God's grace. Christ became an ordinary man to swap places with ordinary people like us. Christ volunteered to be treated like me so that I can be treated like him. As our representative He suffered the punishment for our sin on the cross so that we can be blessed with the benefits of his obedience in heaven. He has died our death and given us his life.

Grace is God's loving gift of salvation in Christ – justification (acceptance) by grace alone through faith alone in Christ alone according to Scripture alone – the slogans of the great Reformers.

Paul later told these Ephesians that we are, by nature, spiritually dead – enslaved and bound by the ways of this world, the influence of Satan within and the sinful desires of our nature. Imagine that we were dead bodies, floating down a river towards a waterfall to be dashed to pieces. But because of His incredible love for us, 'God who is rich in mercy', recognising the corpse of his enemies, sent His own beloved Son into this putrid river to die and so save our lifeless bodies. He gave us mouth-to-mouth resuscitation to restore us to life, clothed and fed us and then welcomed us into His home and His family as beloved sons! This is the gospel of God's grace to which pastors must testify.

A younger preacher once fairly rebuked me for too much challenge in my preaching. 'You're challenging people to more effort but not reassuring them of God's grace', he said. He was right.

People can hear us to say, 'serve harder, lust less, pray more, sin less, evangelise more, worry less, give more, complain less' without the constant encouragement of the gospel of God's grace. We must counter the natural religious instincts of our hearts that quickly revert to thinking either that we are saved by our upright living and ministry, or that we're doomed because of our sin and failures.

Some of us – perhaps because we're from a religious background or are part of an over-zealous first generation of believers – may tend to fall back from teaching grace into teaching religious law. Others of us – perhaps from a secular background or from an over-casual second generation of believers – may tend to fall back from teaching grace into teaching licence or immorality. Whatever the temptation, the faithful pastor knows that the remedy for legalism and licence is the grace of God that teaches us to say 'no' to ungodliness.

A good pastor will apply the doctrines of grace to the personal lives of his hearers. – issues of guilt for wickedness done or experienced in the past, issues of worthlessness and loneliness in the present, and issues of hopelessness and anxiety in facing the future. The gospel of God's grace declares us incredibly precious, totally pardoned and certain of heaven.

### 3. Teach the Kingdom of God!
Read v 25. The Bible has one governing author, the Spirit of God, one principal character, the Son of God and one main theme, the kingdom of God, progressively revealed from beginning to end. For people to understand their place in God's purpose in history, pastors must teach the gospel of the kingdom of God.

In the beginning, God created a paradise kingdom in which His people, Adam and Eve, enjoyed His blessings in His beautiful creation. When they rebelled and were expelled from the Kingdom of God, the human race was condemned with them to live and die outside God's kingdom, in need of a saviour. But God graciously promised Abraham and his descendants a renewed kingdom in which God's people would once more enjoy God's blessing in God's land, and bring blessing to all nations – the gospel promise.

A true pastor will want to show how the history of Israel in the Old Testament shows us that God is a faithful promise-keeper, and yet, how this earthly kingdom of God fell far short of these promises. Throughout Israel's history, prophets warned of the judgment to come, but also promised a glorious new kingdom: a new, international and resurrected people would be redeemed from exile and gathered by God into a new city and creation under a glorious king, servant and Son of Man – a heavenly kingdom of God.

Then there was silence from God for 500 years until a tradesman from Galilee suddenly announced: 'The time has come … the kingdom of God is near. Repent and believe the good news' (Mark 1 v 14, 15).

The king had arrived to open His eternal kingdom to sinners by his death and resurrection. His kingdom is not of this world and we daily pray: *'Your kingdom come'*. But all who surrender to the king become citizens of His heavenly kingdom and await His return. When He comes, His countless people shall be transformed to be like Him, enjoying the glorious garden-city in God's renewed creation with permanent access to the 'tree of life' – the cross of Christ – serving, reigning and singing His praises forever (Rev 21-22). This gospel of the kingdom is the same as the gospel of the King, Jesus Christ our Lord (Acts 28 v 23, 31).

The history of the kingdom of God explains the past, the present and the future, and our place within God's plan to bring all things under Christ's rule. The history of the kingdom is relevant to many massive personal issues we face, especially disappointment and frustration. Our lives and relationships are beset with sin, suffering and sickness because the King has not yet returned. Pastoral ministry involves explaining this kingdom of God – not a boring technical history of Israel, but a personal grasp of where we are in the history of God's King and the arrival of his Kingdom from heaven.

### 4. Teach the whole will of God!

Read v 26-27. Paul gave the elders a balanced diet of Scripture and did not neglect unpopular or difficult parts. Think of how studying the gospels brings us an understanding of the character of Christ, the wisdom literature brings God's insights for decision-making and the prophets bring awareness of the accountability of our lives to God. So, the pastor who preaches mainly from the epistles will leave people with good gospel doctrine, but risks an undernourished love for Jesus, unwise patterns of behaviour and little fear of the Lord! The people of God need a balanced spiritual diet of scripture every bit as urgently as they need a balanced physical diet of salads and fish! A faithful pastor will not merely teach his favourite themes or popular passages but endeavour to give people ' the whole will of God'.

### Blood innocence!

Paul made the most dramatic statement of the day when he said: 'I am innocent of the blood of all men'.

The Elders would immediately have recognised the reference to to Ezekiel 33. The Lord had cautioned the prophet that, if he failed to warn the people of God's judgment, he would be held accountable for the deaths of those he failed to warn, as if spattered with their blood on his clothing.

The elders knew that Paul was urging them not to avoid warning people of the reality of judgment, because this is part of the apostolic gospel. No one would want to face Christ on that day, drenched in the blood of people they failed to warn of the wrath those people must now face. It is striking that, in times of revival, preaching has often been characterised both by a great passion for Christ, and terrifying honesty about the coming judgment.

Teaching about the day of judgment is immensely important for daily life. So many personal problems for Christians are the result of confusion about what God is doing in the world and in our lives. In particular, our experience of injustice, exploitation and suffering can only be understood in the light of the day of judgement. This truth helps us cope with mistreatment and persecution and spurs us on in Evangelism.

Having urged the Elders to emulate his teaching ministry, Paul turns to briefly address two potential threats to the Ephesian church that pastors must face, then and now.

### Protect the church

**Read v 28-31.** There is a guardian element to pastoral ministry which is not popular in a culture that likes to approve of everyone. 'Keep watch over yourselves and all the flock of which the Holy Spirit has made you overseers' He said. Pastors are the greatest potential threat to churches. So they need to provide themselves with ongoing encouragement, accountability and training. 'Be shepherds of the church of God, which he bought with his blood', Paul warned. God's people are immensely precious to Him, and pastors would do well to remember the discipline they will invite from God should they cause any damage to Christ's flock.

'Be shepherds of the church of God' would bring to mind the shocking failures of the Shepherds of Israel on two counts. First, they served themselves rather than the sheep.

> 'Woe to the shepherds of Israel who only take care of themselves... I am against the shepherds and will hold them accountable for my flock...I will rescue my flock ... I will place over them one shepherd, my servant David and he will tend them [ie: Jesus]' **Ezekiel 34 v 2, 22**

The great Pre-Raphaelite painter, Holman-Hunt once depicted the church of his day in these shepherding terms. In a picture entitled, *The Hireling*, the hired shepherd is lying under a haystack with a buxom maid while the neglected sheep have wandered out of the paddock and into other fields and towards a dangerous ravine. Sadly, this could describe many contemporary church 'pastors' who are selfish rather than serving Christ's flock.

Secondly, they proclaimed the delusions of their own minds as the word of God:

> 'Woe to the shepherds who are scattering the sheep of my pasture … They say, 'I had a dream! I had a dream!…those lying prophets who prophesy the delusions of their own minds' **Jeremiah 23 v 1, 25**

Pastors must protect the sheep from all those who would exploit or hurt them. 'I know that after I leave, savage wolves will come in among you and will not spare the flock.' False teaching is not just a healthy debate or a challenging perspective. False teaching damages Christians and tears churches apart like a pack of wolves ripping a carcass apart. I once witnessed a pack of wolves in a game reserve hunt down and tear apart an antelope – it was violent and terrifying. Those who have lived through a church ravaged by false teaching know the carnage that results – not just politically, but personally as people's lives are devastated.

'Even from your own number men will arise and distort the truth in order to draw away disciples after them.' said Paul. 'So be on your guard!' It must have shocked the Ephesians to realise that they themselves could become the false teachers.

False teaching does not openly deny the truth but distorts and twists the truth. The usual motive, observes Paul, is to win a following, usually by reinterpreting Scripture to make it more convenient. Since Ephesus was immoral, pluralistic and proud, the false teachers would easily win a following by questioning whether sex is only for heterosexual marriage, whether salvation is only available through Christ, and whether the unforgiven must go to hell.

But Paul never enjoyed warning against the teaching of others: 'for three years I never stopped warning you night and day with tears'. He was no pedantic heresy-hunter but a pastor who cared for the sheep. Later, in Revelation 2, the Lord Jesus commends the Ephesian church for resisting false apostles, but condemns them for losing 'their first love'. It is certainly possible to become so committed to rooting out false teaching that our love for Christ is neglected and shrivelled.

Lastly, Paul addressed the materialism of Ephesus with enormous pastoral wisdom.

### Give the word!

**Read v 32-35.** Paul knew that the growth of the church was never dependent upon him but upon God, who grows His church through His word: 'Now I commit you to God and to the word of his grace, which can build you up and give you an inheritance among all those who are sanctified'. Since Paul had trained the church to read the Bible for themselves, he could leave them for Jerusalem with confidence that God would continue to build the church

But his final words took a different direction – having reassured them of an inheritance in heaven, he warned them against the acquisition of material wealth on earth. He reminded them of his simple lifestyle and generous spirit, using the farewell words of Samuel:

> 'I have not coveted anyone's silver or gold or clothing. You yourselves know that these hands of mine have supplied my own needs and the needs of my companions. In everything I did, I showed you that by this kind of hard work we must help the weak, remembering the words of the Lord Jesus himself who said, 'It is more blessed to give than to receive'.

Paul was quite distinct from the charlatan roving preachers touting for business and exploiting the crowds. One of the most attractive things about Paul was that he never sponged off the wealthy Ephesians. He didn't favour those with pleasure craft on the harbour or a holiday home on the south coast.

He had accepted manual labour to pay for himself and some of his mission team, to demonstrate that he was giving the gospel because it was true, and not for personal benefit. He'd always encouraged the modest payment of gospel staff to set them free from having to earn a living, but he was clearly encouraging these senior men in a materialistic culture to foster generosity toward the gospel work of the church. They may have been men of substance who owned the houses where the churches met whose support was critical to the expansion of the gospel in the region. Some of them needed to alter their priorities and recognise that God had given them wealth to support gospel work, rather than provide excessive comfort for themselves and their children.

Teach the gospel, Guard the church and Give the word – these are Paul's requirements of elders and leaders who pastor churches in any age and location. In the end, this is like Jesus who taught and warned and gave the word of God at the cost of His life. The apostle Peter wonderfully summarises the themes that Paul taught at Miletus that day:

> Be shepherds of God's flock that is under your care, serving as overseers – not because you must but because you are willing, as God wants you to be; not greedy for money, but eager to serve; not lording it over those entrusted to you, but being examples to the flock. And when the Chief Shepherd appears, you will receive the crown of glory that will never fade away. **1 Peter 5 v 2-4**

The apostle Paul's foundational pastoral ministry to the Gentiles, from which all pastors must learn today, qualifies him without question for inclusion among 'a few good men' for us to admire and emulate.

# BIBLE BACKGROUND

## *The importance of Acts*

The book of Acts is crucial for understanding the apostolic gospel of Christ, the ongoing ministry of Christ's Spirit in His churches, and missionary preaching today.

**The purpose of Acts:** Acts is the companion volume to Luke's Gospel. It describes what Jesus Christ continued to do and teach through His Spirit-empowered apostles. It was compiled from eyewitness accounts (including Luke's own regarding Paul's mission), and written to establish the historical facts of apostolic ministry, and explain the growth of the gospel in the churches.

In particular, Luke wrote to establish the authority of Paul's apostolic ministry, which followed the same pattern as Peter's, and to establish the historical context for Paul's epistles. This is one reason for the lengthy attention to Paul's three missionary journeys. Luke also provided detailed descriptions of Peter and Paul's sermons and ministry, in order to equip the churches of succeeding generations for mission. These descriptions were also important for establishing the law-abiding legitimacy of Christian faith for Christians on trial in Roman courts.

**The theme of Acts:** Acts demonstrates the fulfilment of God's plan of salvation accomplished in the person and work of Christ, as the light for the Gentiles (Isaiah 49 v 6). Through Him, the kingdom of God is opened to the Jews and then the Gentiles. In the Gospel of Luke, this is seen through the death and resurrection of Jesus; in Acts, through the Spirit-empowered apostolic witness, taken up by the churches, to those events. The regular summaries of sermons and speeches proclaim the fulfilment of the Old Testament promises in Christ's death, resurrection, enthronement and giving of the Holy Spirit.

**The problem with Acts:** We must be careful not to adopt, as abiding principles for mission, activity that was unique to the events and circumstances of that time. Much of the text is narrative, and we must be cautious in drawing normative principles from it. The apostles had a unique, foundational ministry. This was the stage of salvation history when the Spirit was first given, and there were many circumstances of mission that were unique to 1st-century culture. We are safest in drawing principles for mission from the teaching, rather than the events of Acts.

All this makes Paul's commendation of his gospel ministry to the Ephesian elders particularly important for Christian mission today.

## Questions for group discussion

1. What is surprising about Paul's description of a pastor's ministry?

2. Does your church preach repentance and faith for salvation?

3. How can we make sure that we not only teach the gospel of grace, but also that this message is heard, rather than a gospel of works?

4. Is your learning from 'the whole counsel of God' something that is applied to everyday life, or does it more naturally fall into the 'academic' category?

5. How can a church be on guard against false teachers?

6. What is the evidence that we really believe that 'it's more blessed to give than to receive'?

# PRAYERFUL EPAPHRAS

*'He is always wrestling in prayer for you'*

COLOSSIANS 4 v 12

*What a friend we have in Jesus,*
*All our sins and griefs to bear!*
*What a privilege to carry*
*Everything to God in prayer!*
*O what peace we often forfeit,*
*O what needless pain we bear –*
*All because we do not carry*
*Everything to God in prayer!*[1]

The Bible everywhere celebrates the wonderful Christian privilege of prayer. It celebrates the God who hears us: 'The eyes of the LORD are on the righteous and his ears are attentive to their cry' (Psalm 34 v 15). It celebrates the benefit of peace to those who pray: 'Do not be anxious about anything, but in everything, by prayer and petition, with thanksgiving, present your requests to God. And the peace of God, which transcends all understanding, will guard your hearts and your minds in Christ Jesus' (Philippians 4 v 6-7). It celebrates the blessings of answered prayer: 'Whatever you ask for in prayer, believe that you have received it, and it will be yours' (Mark 11 v 24). It has rightly been said: 'Prayer is the highest activity of the human soul', and 'Man is at his greatest and highest when, upon his knees, he comes face to face with God'. The Bible boldly celebrates the glorious privilege of prayer.

*So why don't we pray more?*

As the quality of any relationship is determined by the quality of its communication, so, in the individual lives of men and in the history of evangelical Christianity, the periods of closest communion with Jesus Christ have been marked by an appetite for hearing God in the Scriptures, and responding with passionate and expectant prayer. Prayer is like fresh air. Without it we become laboured, weak and unhealthy men.

Yet, sadly, modern surveys of prayer patterns reveal that, on average, Western evangelical Christians pray for about five minutes a day, and their leaders do not pray much longer. Church members often regard the congregational prayer meeting as the most optional rather than the most important. Men who feel far from the LORD commonly admit to chronic prayerlessness. Prayer meetings don't seem to be the boiler rooms of many churches or ministries.

We're all familiar with the excuses. Too busy! Too stressed! Too disappointed to try any more! There are convenient scapegoats in wives, small-group leaders or church pastors who don't inspire us to pray. But most of us recognise that we have become infected with some unhelpful cultural attitudes. There is a godless cynicism which is sceptical that prayer ever works. So we rush around madly trying to change the world ourselves, when change will only come through asking the Lord of the world. There is a sensual apathy in which we crave stimulating entertainment and can't establish the discipline necessary to turn off the television so as to be up in the morning to pray. As a result, we miss out on the deep joy of drawing close to God. There is a relentless socialising that crowds our diaries with an insatiable appetite for relational fulfilment, when such satisfaction is found only in the prayer for which we are now too busy and weary.

It also has to be said that many do live with circumstances that make regular prayer patterns difficult. Disturbed nights with a screaming baby, long hours in a demanding job, intrusive flat-mates or an unsupportive wife can all make prayer difficult.

We know we can't avoid the connection between poor prayer and a poor relationship with God. And, however impressive we may seem in public, we all know the sobering truth of these words: 'What a man is alone on his knees before God, that he is – and no more.' In his *Call to Prayer* J. C. Ryle shrewdly observed: 'I assert confidently that the principal means by which most believers have become great in the church of Christ is the habit of diligent private prayer.' We need help.

Epaphras is not exactly a household name, but Paul's description of his prayer life is an inspiration for us today. We have simple but very helpful first steps in prayer to learn from him.

> Epaphras, who is one of you and a servant of Christ Jesus, sends greetings. He is always wrestling in prayer for you, that you may stand firm in all the will of God, mature and fully assured. I vouch for him that he is working hard for you and for those at Laodicea and Hierapolis. **Colossians 4 v 12-13**

*There was quite a crew with the apostle now, crowding into his cramped, but comfortable prison cell. Paul himself was still chained to the walls, but his condition was much improved with the arrival of his old friend and colleague, Dr Luke. There was the experienced Jewish missionary, Mark (Barnabas' cousin), and his young apprentice, Justus. After Mark's earlier failures, he was now clearly greatly valued and trusted by the apostle. There were Paul's faithful companions, Tychicus and Aristarchus the Macedonian. They'd travelled with Paul on many of his missions. There was Demas from Ephesus, who was, to be honest, a bit worldly and immature, always worried about what people might think.*

*And then there were the two Colossians from the Lycus valley east of Ephesus: Onesimus and Epaphras. Onesimus was both excited and afraid. He'd become a Christian through Paul while* in jail for stealing. Now he was returning home to Colosse with Tychicus to face the music. Paul had written a letter of introduction to his Christian master, Philemon, encouraging him to accept him back as a servant in the household because he'd been born again and was now a brother in Christ.

Epaphras was chained up with Paul. He was very enthusiastic about the planned delegation to Colosse and the Lycus valley because he was from Colosse (he'd been their evangelist and first pastor-teacher) and the delegation was taking a wonderful new epistle specifically for the Colossian church. Epaphras had learned the faith from Paul in Ephesus, and had often returned there for more teaching and training while Paul had lived in Ephesus. He had been arrested with Paul and was now awaiting his own trial. But he didn't mind. It was worth coming, for Paul was addressing the tricky issues in Colosse by letter. It was all about the supremacy of Christ, apparently.

But the most striking thing about Epaphras was how fervently he prayed. Three times a day, as was Paul's Jewish custom, the whole Christian team stopped for prayer. The other prisoners were bemused by these passionate pleas to the God of Israel, and disturbed by the heretical appeals to a God-Man called Jesus Christ. It was obvious why these zealots were in Caesar's prison. Their teaching would seem dangerous to both Jews and Greeks.

But when they prayed, they certainly seemed to mean it. Nothing religious or ceremonial about it; they seemed to pour out their hearts to God. Some of the prisoners were cynical, but many listened intently to these men who didn't seem anywhere near as terrified as most prisoners facing Roman justice.

When Epaphras prayed, he seemed overcome with anguish, pleading with God again and again. Not usually for himself, but for his fellow believers back in Colosse. He almost seemed to be wrestling with God in his soul for these people. Sometimes Epaphras would pray in silence, eyes closed and face screwed up with effort; at other times he'd throw his arms in the air and cry *out loud to God for his house-church and others besides. He was evidently asking that they be kept safe in the message of Christ, standing firm against alternative philosophies. He was anxious that they'd realise how fully blessed they were in knowing this Christ. He asked repeatedly that they would grow up to complete maturity, living like Christ and filled with joy and gladness in the salvation that was theirs in Jesus.*

*The famous apostle Paul seemed to agree thoroughly with all this passionate praying, joining in at every opportunity. He was obviously also very concerned about the Colossians.*

*The time for farewells arrived, and Tychicus and Onesimus were on their way with their letters from Paul, no doubt relieved to be out of the jail and free to travel. When they'd gone, the daily cycle of prayers and discussions resumed. Day after day, they constantly prayed for Christians everywhere. Apparently, their Lord Jesus had done the same!*

---

I understand that the gnu is a noble beast to be found in parts of Africa! It has developed a strategy of charging its enemies from the kneeling position. The gnu derives its impetus to spring forward from its knees. What a sensible beast, and what a fine example for all of us, the gnu would appear to be! For, as we shall see in the case of Epaphras, prayer is the momentum behind a faithful gospel ministry.

Epaphras was from Colosse ('one of you', 4 v 12). He had brought the true gospel of grace to his home town, and, it seems, to the other towns of the Lycus valley, Laodicea and Hierapolis (1 v 7).

Paul warmly commended Epaphras as 'a servant of Christ Jesus', a title of honour he elsewhere applied only to Timothy and himself. He had likewise earlier commended him as 'our dear fellow-servant, who is a faithful minister of Christ on our behalf' (1 v 7).

It's striking that in all Paul's writings he offers only positive commendations of his colleagues. No doubt he corrected them in private and was careful not to flatter with exaggeration; but he understood the need to authenticate reliable gospel workers in order to counter the criticisms of many who disliked the apostolic truth.

Moreover, we know from the epistle to the Colossians that false teachers had arrived in town, belittling Epaphras' teaching of the gospel. These teachers promised much more. So in 1 v 7 Paul had been careful to clarify that Epaphras was a 'fellow-servant', sharing in the same gospel ministry as the apostle; a 'faithful minister' who was reliable and trustworthy; 'of Christ', for, as he explains in the letter, Christ is everything the Colossians could need; 'on our behalf', accurately representing the apostolic ministry entrusted to Paul by Christ Himself. The Colossians needed to recognise that their evangelist-pastor-teacher was reliable, and not be drawn after the novelty of the visiting preachers.

Paul was passing on to the Colossians the greetings of their minister in order to remind them that he loved them, but also to introduce a further telling commendation. Epaphras was constantly praying for them. The faithful church pastor prays constantly for the congregation he serves. There are too many vaunted preachers, leaders and church-planters who simply don't pray for those entrusted to them. Too many respected elders and homegroup leaders don't care enough for their groups to pray for them. May Epaphras teach us to repent of this neglect. There are three vital features of this godly leader's praying which the apostle commends. They concern the 'How', the 'Who' and the 'What' of prayer. He begins by describing 'How' Epaphras prayed.

### He wrestled in prayer!

Paul says Epaphras was regularly 'wrestling', or 'striving', in prayer. The original word is like our word 'agonising'. Clearly, Epaphras was putting enormous effort into praying. He didn't always find it easy and pleasurable. He wasn't relaxing and resting in prayer. He was wrestling!

My sons absolutely love watching WrestleMania's 'SmackDown' on the television, with Bobby Lashly, John Cena, Batista and the Undertaker smashing lumps out of each other in front of screaming crowds (I quite like it too, but don't tell my sons). Even if some of it is staged, the sheer artery-bursting effort that these huge men put into these contests is extraordinary. That is how Epaphras prayed, says Paul. He wrestled in prayer. We are immediately faced with the fact that we just don't try hard enough to pray. We too easily give up because we feel tired or distracted. We need to learn to wrestle and struggle in prayer.

There's nothing unspiritual or ungodly about wrestling in prayer. The same word here translated 'wrestling' is used of Jesus praying earnestly in the garden of Gethsemane on the night before He died. It is also used by Paul of his own ministry in Colossians 1 v 29 and 2 v 1. Paul says: 'To this end I labour, struggling with all his energy, which so powerfully works in me.' The difference between Christian effort and merely human effort is that in the former we ask for strength and depend on the strength of God for the struggle. God's limitless power is available for this. But we access this strength from His Holy Spirit by beginning to wrestle and although it does feel like a struggle, we will find we can do it. Human beings are weak. We get tired, and Satan and our sinful natures drag us down from reaching up to God. If you'd asked Paul or Epaphras how they found prayer, they would clearly have replied: 'Sometimes I find it a great struggle and I have to wrestle in prayer.' But, strengthened by God, wrestling prayer is genuine prayer.

We do know how to wrestle and struggle for other things in life. Many of us wrestle with great determination at work or in sport, or even with a difficult relationship. Jacob (who was renamed Israel) was like that. He was a great schemer and negotiator, who wrestled with his brother Esau and then his Uncle Laban to get what he wanted. But God famously taught him to wrestle with

God for blessing from Him. An angel of God wrestled with Jacob throughout the night, humbling him with a dislocated hip. At daybreak, Jacob fought on:

> 'I will not let you go unless you bless me.' The man asked him, 'What is your name?' 'Jacob,' he answered. Then the man said, 'Your name will no longer be Jacob, but Israel [meaning he struggles with God], because you have struggled with God and with men and have overcome.' **Genesis 32 v 22-28**

When was the last time we wrestled in prayer all night like that?

It was as if God were saying to Jacob, and all His people after him, including us: "You struggle and wrestle for so much in life – now come and wrestle and struggle with Me; engage with Me in prayer that I may bless you! You talk on your mobile to so many people who can't help. Come and talk to Me! Wrestle with Me for My blessings." God does not want to be merely the hidden financial backer, secretly bankrolling our enterprises. He is our Father, who, amazingly, wants to help us, personally and tenderly, through each day.

A good father doesn't simply produce cash when his son demands it, as if the cash is of no value. A good father will want his son to explain *why* he needs the money to help the boy realise that this will cost his father, who thinks carefully about providing it, before giving it out of kindness. God is the best kind of father, and He wants us to persuade Him in prayer and not just demand as if He were a vending machine.

The great Puritan Christians urged that prayer be a seeking after sweet enjoyment of personal communion with God, for which great fervency and effort was required. Thomas Brooks contrasted the intensity of 'the heavenly fire, the holy fervency' of real prayer with 'feeble prayers' and 'cold prayers' that are ineffective, like birds with broken wings that cannot fly up to heaven.[2] He writes of this verse about Epaphras' praying: 'It notes the vehemency and fervour of Epaphras' prayers for the Colossians. Look as the wrestlers do ... strain every joint in their bodies, that they may be victorious; so Epaphras did ... strain every joint of his soul, if I may so speak, that he might be victorious with God upon the Colossians' account.'

Like Jacob and the Puritans, Epaphras had learned to wrestle and struggle in prayer, and we must learn to do the same.

The second feature of Epaphras' praying that the apostle commends concerns 'Who' he wrestled in prayer for.

## He wrestled in prayer for others!

Most of us can manage some prayer for ourselves, but praying for others is more difficult because we are naturally self-absorbed and self-concerned. We can learn from Epaphras something of how to intercede with God for other people.

### *His prayer was intercessory.*

Paul says Epaphras was wrestling in prayer 'for you', literally 'on behalf of you'.

This was not, of course, to suggest that Epaphras had taken up a priestly role to replace Christ's work of interceding with the Father to maintain their salvation. 'Christ Jesus, who died – more than that, who was raised to life – is at the right hand of God and is also interceding for us' (Romans 8 v 34). The Roman Catholic idea that a clergyman intercedes with God for the salvation of others is quite wrong, since Christ alone is our sacrificial High Priest: '... because Jesus lives for ever, he has a permanent priesthood. Therefore he is able to save completely those who come to God through him, because he always lives to intercede for them' (Hebrews 7 v 24-25). Our prayers cannot guarantee the salvation of others – that is Christ's unique ministry.

Neither did Epaphras pray to improve the prayers of others. It is the Holy Spirit's role to translate our prayers to accord with the will of the Father: 'The Spirit helps us in our weakness. We do not know what we ought to pray for, but the Spirit himself intercedes for us with groans that words cannot express ... the Spirit intercedes for the saints in accordance with God's will' (Romans 8 v 26-27). Our prayers cannot improve the prayers of others – that is the Holy Spirit's unique ministry.

But Epaphras could and did pray for the needs of others as well as his own. We find this commended everywhere in Scripture. Jesus taught us to ask our Father for our daily bread, the forgiveness of our sins and to deliver us from evil, for all the people of God, not just for ourselves. The apostle Paul begins most of his letters with full reports of what he prays for his readers. We are not only individual sons of God, we are also brothers within the family and people of God. As the great theologian John Calvin put it: 'There is nothing in which we can benefit our brethren more than in commending them to the providential care of the best of Fathers.'[3]

And in this humble hidden ministry, we can help change the world, for we pray to the Ruler of the world. As the great 18th-century American theologian Jonathan Edwards (not a British triple jumper) is reported to have said: 'There is no way that Christians in a private capacity can do so much to promote the work of God and advance the kingdom of Christ as by prayer.'

Some Christians use a weekly diary with the initials of those for whom they pray written against each day. I have one friend who uses the *Operation World* year-long diary with names against each country, according to their birthdays. I am honoured to be prayed for along with Bangladesh! Whatever system he used, Epaphras had learnt to intercede for others, and we must do the same.

### His prayer was preventative

It is striking that Epaphras was praying for a church before it was in crisis. From what Paul has heard from Epaphras about the Colossians he writes: 'I ... delight to see how orderly you are and how firm your faith in Christ is' (2 v 5). Yet we then hear that Epaphras is praying that they may 'stand firm' (4 v 12). He was worried about the impact of false teaching upon the church. But he didn't wait until the church was melting in the heat of division and controversy. He was praying beforehand, preventatively, rather than after tragedy had struck.

How often we turn to prayer when it's too late, when a friend or church has already collapsed rather than when they are still standing firm. Prevention is better than cure, and we need to pray for strong and sound Christians and churches to remain so, rather than merely pray for those who've crumbled already. After all, Satan's attacks are surely launched more severely upon those strong in the faith of the gospel than upon those who have already abandoned it. We cannot take the faithfulness of others for granted, even if they are senior saints or established ministers. Let us be careful to pray preventatively for people, churches, ministries, colleges and preachers who are being used by God, that He will continue to protect and provide for them.

### His prayer was sustained
It is also striking that Epaphras was 'always' (meaning regularly) wrestling in prayer for the Colossians. Not 'sometimes' or even 'often', but 'always'! Paul had earlier encouraged the Colossians to 'devote [themselves] to prayer' (4 v 2). Jesus Himself 'often withdrew to lonely places and prayed' (Luke 5 v 16), and from the account of His time in the garden of Gethsemane, where we read that 'he went away and prayed the same thing' (Mark 14 v 39), we may assume that He often prayed for things more than once. Paul himself prayed three times for his 'thorn in the flesh' to be removed.

When Jesus condemned pagan 'babbling' in His Sermon on the Mount, He was teaching against 'empty phrases', repeated in order to manipulate God, with no earnest request from the heart. He was not teaching against all repetition or genuine use of liturgy, but against the mindless repetition of prayers, such as does go on in some traditional churches and pagan temples. But with heartfelt requests, Paul commanded the Thessalonians, 'pray continually' (1 Thessalonians 5 v 17). This is because prayer is not like lodging a tax return with the Inland Revenue once a year, but like talking to Dad over breakfast and tea every day. Prayer is not a technicality, but a relationship. Epaphras understood this, so he kept on wrestling in prayer.

How often, when people become Christians, we discover that somewhere in the wider family or community, someone has been faithfully praying for them for decades! A friend of mine, Andy Hawthorne of The Message and Eden Project Ministries in schools and housing estates around Manchester, tells of how he learned about the blessing of sustained prayer. After his schools outreach had become quite a sensation in Manchester, regularly filling the Apollo Concert Hall for their 'Planet Life' rap and gospel shows, he was invited to meet some little old ladies from his church in Cheadle who had been praying for him. When he went to meet them he was completely humbled to discover that they had been regularly meeting on Friday nights, praying for him to become a Christian and now for his ministry team for many, many years. He now understood why his ministry had prospered. One of them said to Andy: 'Don't ever give up on prayer. I was praying all my life for my husband to become a Christian, and the old beggar was finally born again when he was 99 years old – so never give up!' Like Epaphras, those elderly saints understood the value of sustained prayer.

The third feature of Epaphras' praying that the apostle commends concerns 'What' he wrestled in prayer for.

### He wrestled in prayer for others to stand firm!

Too often we pray for superficial blessings, even for our own wives and children. 'Please help her cough to get better and his exam to go well'! When we pray for our church, we pray that the money will be raised, the pastor refreshed by his holidays and the home-groups have happy away-days. When we pray for the nations of the world, we pray for wars to cease, wisdom for G8 leaders, human rights abuses to stop and even for freedom for gospel preaching. All good things, but we rarely pray for any specific spiritual needs.

Contrast that with Paul's summary of Epaphras' prayer requests: 'that you may stand firm in all the will of God, mature and fully assured.' When read in the context of the letter, we discover that these are the specific spiritual needs of that church. Indeed, this prayer captures the theme of Paul's letter. Unsurprisingly, the deepest longings of this pastor's heart formed the burden of the apostle's letter.

### *He prayed that they might 'stand firm'*

In the letter, we discover Paul telling the Colossians not to be deceived by 'fine-sounding arguments' (2 v 4). What sort of teaching could rock this well-taught church? It all becomes clear in chapter 2. The Colossians were in danger from those who would capture them with their human philosophy (v 8), judge them by their religious observance (v 16) and disqualify them with their visionary experiences (v 18). This mixture of new teachings was characterised by wanting to add to the Christ of the gospel that Epaphras had taught them.

The three strands described here sound remarkably like what we would call liberalism, Roman Catholicism and extreme charismaticism; they are nothing new, but simply the ancient offers of human rational thinking, religious tradition and personal experience that have always unsettled gospel churches. Paul's response was to urge the Colossians: 'So then, just as you received Christ Jesus as Lord [the gospel], continue to live in him, rooted and built up in him, strengthened in the faith as you were taught, and overflowing with thankfulness' (2 v 6-7); ie: stand firm in the gospel of Christ. Paul was writing about what Epaphras was praying about.

We too should be praying that our Christian friends and our churches will stand firm against the beguiling additions of liberalism, Roman Catholicism and charismaticism to supplement Christ with their reason, tradition and experience. Instead of praying that our children will be safe from colds and poor grades, perhaps we could pray for safety from false teaching, as Epaphras did.

### He prayed that they would stand firm '*in all the will of God*'

Epaphras prayed that his church would be literally 'filled with everything that is God's will'. 'Fullness' has been a big theme in Paul's letter. The new teachers were apparently offering greater spiritual fullness to the Colossians than Epaphras had seemed to offer. So after reporting his prayers in chapter 1, Paul has been explaining that Christ is everything. He summarises: 'God was pleased to have all his fullness dwell in [Christ]' (1 v 19). In response to each of the heresies, Paul talks about the fullness of Christ. To human philosophy he replies: 'For in Christ all the fullness of the Deity lives in bodily form, and you have been given fullness in Christ' (2 v 9-10).

To religious condemnation he responds: 'These are a shadow of the things that were to come; the reality, however, is found in Christ' (2 v 17). To visionary experiences he responds: 'Such a person goes into great detail about what he has seen, and his unspiritual mind puffs him up with idle notions. He has lost connection with the Head' (2 v 18-19). Paul is showing that to have Christ is to have all of God. If we have Christ, we lack nothing. This is again what Epaphras was praying – that the Colossians would know they were filled with everything that God willed for them in the Spirit of Christ.

We, too, need to pray for our families and churches that they will appreciate the fullness of God that is theirs in Christ.

### He prayed that they would become '*mature and fully assured*'

Epaphras was praying that his church would be, literally, 'complete and fully assured'. Again, Paul has been explaining that wholeness, perfection and completion are to be found in Christ, and not in human philosophy, religious observance or ecstatic experiences. He describes his own ministry in these terms: 'We proclaim him [Christ], admonishing and teaching everyone with all wisdom, so that we may present everyone perfect [complete] in Christ. To this end I labour, struggling ...' (1 v 28-29). In contrast to the persuasive new teachers, Paul taught Christ from the Scriptures in order that his hearers might become like Christ in all His perfection, and to this aim he carried on struggling. This is precisely what Epaphras was wrestling in prayer for (as well as wrestling in teaching) – that his church family might become more like Jesus; that instead of being unsettled by those who promised something more, they would be assured that, in Christ, they had everything of God.

We too need to pray that our families and churches will become complete, living like Christ, assured and contented with Him. Let's not just pray for superficial blessings like happiness, health and exams. Let's pray for specific spiritual needs. Let Christ be the content of our prayers for our children, churches and governments. That is what Epaphras was praying for.

Epaphras teaches us how to pray: wrestling with God. He teaches us who to pray for: other people. He teaches us what to pray for: Christ-likeness. Unless we learn to wrestle in prayer for others and to stand firm in Christ, our lives and our churches will remain shrivelled. In his published research on the remarkable work of God in China over recent years, *China's Christian Millions*, Tony Lambert identifies prayer as one of the lessons we must learn (alongside the authority of Scripture, obedience, repentance and seriousness, where I suspect we are not so weak). He observes:'The Chinese revival is saturated in prayer, and often prayer with groaning and tears.' It is common, apparently, to organise not only prayer meetings for many hours during the night, but continuous prayer so that members of churches are allotted times of the day to pray wherever they are, so that continuous prayer is offered to God. Praying like that is what the apostle commends as 'working hard' for the Christians of Colosse, Laodicea and Hierapolis. Perhaps we ought to recognise that prayer is hard work as well as a delightful privilege that must be practised regularly. For his faithful wrestling in prayer that others might be assured in Christ, little-known Epaphras belongs among 'a few good men'!

## BIBLE BACKGROUND

### *Colossians*

Though it is evident that Paul wrote Colossians from prison, we don't know which prison. Traditionally it was held to have been in Rome, but good arguments can be advanced for Ephesus, and in the end it doesn't really matter.

What is plain is that Epaphras had brought to Paul reports of theological problems caused by those offering the Colossians distracting supplements to their faith in the gospel of Christ. Some blend of Greek philosophy, Jewish traditions and local superstition was threatening to 'deceive you by fine-sounding arguments' (2 v 4). These teachers were threatening to:

- take the Colossians captive with 'hollow and deceptive philosophy, which depends on human tradition and the basic principles of this world rather than on Christ' (2 v 8);
- judge the Colossians by 'what you eat or drink, or with regard to a religious festival, a New Moon celebration or a Sabbath day' (2 v 16);
- disqualify the Colossians with 'false humility and the worship of angels' (2 v 18).

The answer to these supplements was to teach the supremacy of Christ and the fullness of God in Him. The message of the letter is summarised in 2 v 6-7: 'So then, just as you received Christ Jesus as Lord, continue to live in him, rooted and built up in him, strengthened in the faith as you were taught, and overflowing with thankfulness.' Paul's theme is simply: 'Stand firm in Christ; He is all you need!'

The Colossians were currently stable, but were threatened by those who diminish the fullness and supremacy of Christ. So Paul wrote to commend Christ, and Epaphras wrestled in prayer for them to stand firm in Him.

## Questions for group discussion

1. How could we encourage one another to wrestle in prayer more?

2. How could we encourage one another to pray for others more?

3. How could we encourage one another to pray more about standing firm in Christ?

### *References*

1 *What a friend we have in Jesus*, Joseph Scriven (1819-86).

2 Thomas Brooks, *'The Privy Keep of Heaven'* in Works II, p258-259.

3 John Calvin, *'Prayer'*, in Institutes of Christian Religion, Westminster John Knox Press, 1997, p60.

# 10 LOYAL ONESIPHORUS

*'He often refreshed me and was not ashamed of my chains'*

2 TIMOTHY 1 v 16

Being loyal to someone else requires a sacrificial devotion to others that we often find difficult, especially if our association with them is costly.

Being a Christian means being loyal to Christ. Jesus said: 'If anyone is ashamed of me and my words in this adulterous and sinful generation, the Son of Man will be ashamed of him when he comes in his Father's glory' (Mark 8 v 38). In his second letter to Timothy, the apostle Paul makes it clear to his beloved colleague that loyalty to Jesus is expressed in loyalty to the gospel of Jesus and to those who proclaim the gospel of Jesus. By contrast with so many who had deserted him and his gospel, Paul commends to Timothy a little-known friend of his who had shown wonderful loyalty to him and the gospel of Christ. We may not know how to pronounce his name, but we all have much to learn from the loyalty of Onesiphorus.

> What you heard from me, keep as the pattern of sound teaching, with faith and love in Christ Jesus. Guard the good deposit that was entrusted to you – guard it with the help of the Holy Spirit who lives in us.
>
> You know that everyone in the province of Asia has deserted me, including Phygelus and Hermogenes.
>
> May the Lord show mercy to the household of Onesiphorus, because he often refreshed me and was not ashamed of my chains. On the contrary, when he was in Rome, he searched hard for me until he found me. May the Lord grant that he will find mercy from the Lord

175

on that day! You know very well in how many ways he helped me in Ephesus.

You then, my son, be strong in the grace that is in Christ Jesus. And the things you have heard me say in the presence of many witnesses entrust to reliable men who will also be qualified to teach others.

**2 Timothy 1 v 13 – 2 v 2**

*Conditions were truly awful. Prisoners were chained to the wall with iron manacles that chafed at bloodied ankles. Some were ill with dysentery, others badly beaten. The stench of human excrement in fetid air was nauseating. The constant noise of clanking chains punctuated with cries of pain and anguished sobbing made any sleep nearly impossible. Once a day, the guards brought the only meal, a thin gruel. If someone had died during the night, they'd unlock the gate into the nearby sewer and tip the body in. For a few of the prisoners there might sometimes be a frightened family member visiting with extra food and basic provisions, briefly exchanging desperate whispers before being ushered away. The apostle Paul had been under open house arrest before, but this gloomy underground dungeon, somewhere in Rome, was truly barbaric. Such prisons, holding criminals awaiting execution, were notoriously dreadful, and once thrown in, few came out alive.*

*At his first hearing on charges of causing civil unrest, absolutely no one had turned up to speak in Paul's defence. So now he was waiting to be sentenced to death. He'd been waiting months now, surrounded by hardened criminals, the scum of the Roman Empire. His hair and beard had grown long and matted, his body emaciated from malnutrition. Cold and alone, he pondered the vulnerable state of the little house churches he'd planted in the provinces of Asia (Turkey), Macedonia and Achaia (northern and southern Greece), and prayed.*

*He'd been beaten, stoned or flogged many times before. He was familiar with shipwreck and persecution. Hunger, thirst and sleepless nights had become normal for Christ's apostle to the Gentiles, as he followed his Master down the way of the cross. But there was so much more he'd hoped to do. He'd left so many young and inexperienced teachers and elders in charge of the churches. So many Gentile nations still unreached. He would never now fulfil his ambition to conduct a mission to Spain.*

*How could no one turn up as a character witness for him at his trial? As soon as he'd been arrested this time, his support just seemed to drain away like rain on dry soil. He was learning what it had felt like for Jesus that Thursday night when everyone deserted Him, too. Even the well-known rising star preachers, Phygelus and Hermogenes, had abandoned him. Presumably, they thought he'd been too provocative, been unwise in his language, picked the wrong issue or had it coming to him – the usual excuses.*

*Apparently Demas had gone to Thessalonica. Such an able young man with so much potential. No doubt everyone thought this a great appointment to such a prestigious church team. But Paul knew it was really because Demas had fallen in love with this world and wanted an honourable ministry. Crescens had fled to Galatia and even Titus had gone to Dalmatia. No doubt they'd found plausible reasons. Perhaps they'd pleaded 'academic research' or the 'I'll be able to do so much more from safety in the years to come' arguments. Paul had heard them all before. But deserting Paul in his hour of need didn't bode well for their faithfulness to his gospel in the future.*

*Thankfully, faithful as always, the Lord Himself had strengthened Paul to proclaim the gospel boldly at his hearing. Despite the ignorant hostility of his accusers, he'd known remarkable peace protecting his heart. But now that his 'departure' to glory seemed certain, how would the baton of gospel ministry ever be passed on to the next generation? If only he could talk to Timothy, his beloved younger colleague leading the church he'd planted in*

*Ephesus. If only he could gather his mission team one last time to plan the continuation of the Lord's work after his death. If only one of the brothers could find him! Appeals to the guards were proving fruitless. And so he prayed and quietly sang hymns and waited. And waited.*

*Until one day, one fantastic, glorious day, Onesiphorus found him. He nearly hadn't spotted him, Paul being so thin and his hair so long and clothes so tattered, and being so distracted by the nauseating stench. But as visitor and prisoner slowly recognised each other through the gloom, these old friends had embraced and wept with unrestrained joy to see each other again. Onesiphorus couldn't stay long that first visit. But he came every day thereafter for ages, bringing food, writing materials and soon friends like Eubulus, Pudens, Linus, Claudia and others in Rome he knew less well, and eventually he even brought his faithful colleague Dr Luke. His medical help was so welcome.*

*So things were more bearable now. How Paul thanked God for Onesiphorus. He wasn't a great preacher or teacher (Paul remembered that dreadful sermon in Ephesus when they all realised that teaching definitely wasn't his thing). No matter – Christ had given plenty of others to teach. He was no scholar or strategist or musician either. No, but Onesiphorus was a wonderfully loyal friend – the best friend a gospel man could ever want. Ever since he and his family had been born again in Ephesus, they'd proved to be such wonderful supporters of Paul and his ministry. And when it mattered most, when all that they'd worked towards seemed near to collapse, when everyone else turned and ran for cover, Onesiphorus risked everything to find his apostle in that disgusting dungeon in faraway Rome. You could always count on Onesiphorus. He'd stayed in Rome as long as he could to support this preacher of Christ. He was worth his weight in gold. Loyal Onesiphorus – every preacher needs one.*

*And now, with Luke daily bringing provisions, parchments and candles, Paul had been able to dictate a stirring last epistle for*

Timothy, his beloved son in the faith. This letter was an urgent call for loyalty to the apostle's gospel ministry in the light of his impending death. It could be summarised by the two appeals at the beginning and end: 'Do not be ashamed to testify about our Lord, or ashamed of me his prisoner. But join with me in suffering for the gospel, by the power of God' (1 v 8); and 'Preach the Word; be prepared in season and out of season; correct, rebuke and encourage – with great patience and careful instruction' (4 v 2).

The letter also urged Timothy to try to come to visit him, with Mark (and to bring a warm cloak and some parchments for their mission planning), before his execution. His themes in the letter covered the inevitability of gospel teachers suffering persecution, the danger of popular but worldly church leaders like Hymenaeus and Alexander (who denied the bodily resurrection of Christ and the need for godliness), the rewards for faithful Christian service being primarily in the world to come and, above all, the need to keep teaching the apostolic gospel of the Scriptures.

He urged Timothy: 'What you heard from me, keep as the pattern of sound teaching, with faith and love in Christ Jesus. Guard the good deposit that was entrusted to you – guard it with the help of the Holy Spirit who lives in us' (1 v 13-14). These words contained the parallel charges concerning Paul's gospel teaching – keep it as the pattern or model of teaching, and guard it as a sacred treasure for the generations to come. Timothy must resolve to be loyal to the apostolic faith amid all the defections to false teaching that the Lord had told them to expect. The future expansion of the kingdom of God depended upon such loyalty, not only from Timothy, but from generations of pastors after him, for whom Paul hoped he was also writing. So Paul had contrasted the disloyalty of everyone else in Asia (the leaders who should have known better) with the loyalty to Paul and his gospel shown by Onesiphorus.

He warned Timothy of the chilling facts he already knew: 'You know that everyone in the province of Asia has deserted me, *including Phygelus and Hermogenes' (1 v 15). Of course, he didn't mean every individual in the province (after all, Timothy and the church in Ephesus were still loyal). But the overseer-bishops who should have been setting an example were abandoning his teaching at every point where they were under pressure to be politically correct.*

*He was being painted as sexist because of his teaching concerning the creation doctrines of male headship in the family and the church (despite half the members of his ministry teams being women). He was accused of intolerant bigotry because of his insistence upon the uniqueness of Christ's incarnation, redemption and resurrection, and his denial that Jews or anyone else could be saved outside of Christ (Jesus had plainly said that no one comes to the Father but by Him).*

*He was condemned as homophobic for clarifying Jesus' teaching on marriage that condemned all sexual activity outside heterosexual marriage (even though these leaders knew that such lifestyles would send people to hell). Instead of standing up for him, they protected their own reputations with such impervious rhetoric that Paul was left isolated and despised.*

*But Onesiphorus was different. Onesiphorous expressed his loyalty to Christ and the gospel in his loyalty to those who taught it. How Paul thanked God for loyal men like Onesiphorus. As Paul finally entrusted his scroll-epistle to Luke for sending to Timothy, the two friends embraced. 'I miss him, you know, my loyal old friend Onesiphorus,' said Paul. 'He was always such a refreshing encouragement.'*

*'To be sure,' agreed Luke. 'Full of the Spirit, that man.' He paused. 'Only trouble was, I never could work out how to pronounce his name!'*

Onesiphorus demonstrated his loyalty to Jesus in three kinds of loyalty shown towards his former pastor, the apostle Paul, from which we can all learn today.

### He often refreshed Paul!

'May the Lord show mercy to the household of Onesiphorus, because he often refreshed me' (1 v 16). He had often 'refreshed', or revived and uplifted, Paul. Although the apostle must primarily have been thinking of the recent refreshments in prison, his reference to the household back in Ephesus before talking of Onesiphorus' arrival in Rome suggests that this ministry of refreshment went back to Paul's time in Ephesus. Onesiphorus and his family were one of those supportive families that are such a blessing to gospel ministers everywhere, even when they aren't yet in prison (though the way European legislation is going, it may not be too long before gospel teachers will be in prison for their faithfulness to Scripture, and will certainly need refreshment-visiting then).

Over my own years of paid ministry, I can think of such special families who have invited my family to lunch, sent encouraging cards, offered to babysit, cooked numerous meals during the prolonged illness of a child, paid off a burdensome overdraft, offered us a weekend break, repeatedly thanked me for sermons even when they knew they were seriously flawed, etc, etc. I know that others have also experienced their generosity and hospitality. Their kindnesses to us have been their expression of loyalty to the gospel, and they will never know how refreshing they have been at times when I was exhausted and discouraged.

I think that some church members and families may not realise how refreshing they could be. The more glamorous gifts of teaching and leading are often nowhere near as important to the continuing faithfulness of a gospel ministry as the encouraging ministries of 'refreshment' in the loyal spirit of Onesiphorus. I'm convinced that many preachers drift away from the apostolic faith, not because they want to abandon ship, but through sheer discouragement. If only Onesiphorus had been in their church to refresh them.

## He wasn't ashamed of Paul!

Secondly, Paul writes that he 'was not ashamed of my chains' (1 v 16). It was so important that Timothy, and all preachers and teachers after him, learn not to be ashamed of the gospel of Christ and those who preach it. Disloyalty to the faithful preacher almost invariably leads to disloyalty to the faith. Onesiphorus risked not only the shame and disgrace of being associated with the despised apostle. He also risked being arrested and punished with him. But his loyalty to Jesus made him loyal to the preachers of Jesus.

Again, I can think of wonderful men like that. Our congregations recently resolved to make a stand for the faith of the Scriptures by declaring ourselves in temporarily impaired communion with our diocesan bishop, because he refused to publicly uphold the Bible's teaching on sexual morality. It was a carefully considered decision taken only after much prayer and consultation with other evangelical leaders. I don't want to revisit the issues now. But the day after our elders and staff unanimously agreed to stand against the bishop, our senior elder, a wise, godly and much-respected man of peaceful disposition, sent me the most encouraging postcard. It simply said:

> Dear Richard, After our momentous decision yesterday, I am writing to tell you that we, the laymen, are 100% behind you. No doubt there will be debates about timing and tactics but I want you to know that you can count on our total support. Yours sincerely...

I can't tell you how encouraging that expression of support was to me. In the event, I had my licence removed by the Bishop and had to pursue a legal process to be reinstated, but throughout it all, he and all the other leaders and congregations stood shoulder to shoulder with me. It wasn't just leaders, but the encouragement and loyalty of countless church members that was so encouraging. The truth is that I couldn't have done it without them, and I thank God for them.

And there were others too – among them Vaughan, William, Hugh, Jonathan and especially Paul – senior church leaders who have suffered great criticism for their support, but should be honoured for expressing their loyalty to the gospel in their loyalty to a gospel teacher. Not everyone will agree with what we did. But we can all learn from the loyalty of those who stood up to be counted as part of their loyalty to Christ. That is the spirit of Onesiphorus, and I wonder whether some leading members of churches don't realise how much their expressions of unashamed loyalty would strengthen their preachers to take up Jude's charge to 'contend for the faith that was once for all entrusted to the saints. For certain men whose condemnation was written about long ago have secretly slipped in among you. They are godless men, who change the grace of our God into a licence for immorality and deny Jesus Christ our only sovereign and Lord' (Jude 3-4). It was vital that Timothy learn from the example of Onesiphorus to remain unashamed of the gospel and support those who preached it. That is the spirit of Onesiphorus.

## He helped Paul in many ways!
Thirdly, Paul says: 'You know very well in how many ways he helped me in Ephesus' (1 v 18). Well, Timothy clearly knew, but we don't. And we don't need to. The point is that Onesiphorus was helpful in all sorts of ways – in whatever way he could help. How wonderful to have had a man like him and a family like his in the church! They were always looking for ways in which to be helpful. I expect they were first to sign up for the stewarding rota, first to commit to the annual house party, first to contribute finance sacrificially, first at the monthly prayer meeting and always with positive appreciation to offer.

What a joy such people are to every gospel preacher. They are a miracle of God's grace, fashioned by God to assist the preaching of the gospel. Allow me to say to any who are reading this and who know that this is their ministry, on behalf of preachers everywhere, 'Thank you!' Please don't let anyone make you feel second-rate because you are not a leader or a preacher. Others can do that job. Your ministry of refreshment, unashamed loyalty to the biblical faith and general helpfulness is absolutely vital to the spread of the gospel. In our church-planting strategy, we have discovered that, in addition to some people, a venue, a leader and some money, it is absolutely imperative to have an Onesiphorus as an elder, alongside the preacher. We have found that it is vital to have someone normal who models unshakeable loyalty to the gospel and those who preach it, if the new church is to thrive. This is the character of Onesiphorus.

No wonder Paul wishes the mercy of the Lord Jesus to be shown both upon his household (1 v 16) and upon him on the day of judgement (1 v 18). Paul deliberately wishes that, just as Onesiphorus 'found' him, so Onesiphorus will 'find' mercy from the Lord. The separation of these hopes for the man and his family prompts the conclusion that Onesiphorus and his household were still separated (perhaps even that Onesiphorus had died – though there is no warrant to justify prayer for the dead from this verse). It was costly for the whole family for Onesiphorus to be so supportive, just as it is often costly today for a man to lead by example in loyal support of gospel teaching. Paul had good grounds for thinking that the Lord Jesus would be very approving of Onesiphorus' kindness to Paul in his need, especially in prison, for Jesus had explicitly said that kindness to His people is regarded by Him as kindness to Himself:

> Then the King will say to those on his right, 'Come, you who are blessed by my Father; take your inheritance, the kingdom prepared for you since the creation of the world. For I was hungry and you gave me something to eat, I was thirsty and you gave me something to drink, I was a stranger and you invited me in, I needed clothes and you clothed me, I was sick and you looked after me, I was in prison

> and you came to visit me. Whatever you did for one of the least of
> these brothers of mine, you did for me.' **Matthew 25 v 34-40**

It is striking that, having contrasted the disloyalty of everyone else in Asia with the loyalty of Onesiphorus, Paul then resumes his theme with Timothy: 'You then, my son, be strong in the grace that is in Christ Jesus. And the things you have heard me say in the presence of many witnesses entrust to reliable men who will also be qualified to teach others' (2 v 1-2). It seems obvious that Paul expects the example of Onesiphorus, who was well known to Timothy, to inspire him to be similarly loyal to the apostolic faith.

Perhaps he is also clarifying that, in seeking 'reliable' men to whom he should entrust the sacred treasure of the gospel to teach to successive generations, Timothy should be careful to choose men of loyalty like Onesiphorus. It will be vital to pick men who are not only able (to teach) but also reliable (loyal to the gospel). And, above all, Paul wanted to assure Timothy that the strength that made Onesiphorus so loyal was not unique to him or a secret that we can't know. It is found 'in the grace that is in Christ Jesus' (2 v 1) and 'the help of the Holy Spirit who lives in us' (1 v 14), which is available to all believers who pray for it. We can all ask God to help us become loyal.

## Support those who are imprisoned for the faith

Perhaps, finally, we learn from Onesiphorus the importance of supporting those who are imprisoned for their faith. Paul was certainly not the last Christian to suffer torture and imprisonment while awaiting unjust execution. The epistle to the Hebrews says:

> Remember those in prison as if you were their fellow-prisoners, and
> those who are ill-treated as if you yourselves were suffering.
>
> **Hebrews 13 v 3**

Let us be willing to pray, lobby, give for and visit those who are imprisoned for the faith.

In this country, we may want to be involved in one of the many prison ministries that bring support and the gospel to inmates (and try to protect Christian ministries from the kind of restrictions imposed recently upon the Inner Change ministry in Dartmoor prison for reasons of secular diversity policies). Further afield, let us be sure to support organisations like Barnabas Fund, Christian Solidarity Worldwide and Release International, which work to give compassionate support to persecuted Christians around the world. In Pakistan, for example, Christians crammed into the overcrowded, disease-infested prisons built by the British are apparently often systematically tortured. Sohail, a Release International prison visitor in Pakistan, has helped to distribute hundreds of parcels to the devastated families of these prisoners, and is working with the Centre for Legal Assistance and Settlement for the release of Christians falsely accused of blasphemy. Sohail observes: 'Nobody supports the families. Even churches, even organisations, even the government doesn't provide the support, like finances or food. No pastor wants to visit the family for prayer.' So Sohail does it, in the spirit of Onesiphorus. Christians all over the world need loyal men like Onesiphorus.

For his loyalty, Onesiphorus joins 'a few good men'.

## BIBLE BACKGROUND

### *1 Timothy*

This letter is a stirring call from the great apostle Paul to his experienced and faithful apprentice and colleague Timothy, now working in the strategic church in Ephesus, to remain loyal to the apostolic gospel for which Paul was suffering. It's plain that Paul was in chains in prison, probably in Rome, expecting to be executed shortly as a criminal. This letter is full of repeated calls to carry on his gospel ministry 'for the sake of the elect, that they too may obtain the salvation that is in Christ Jesus' (2 v 10). Paul was concerned to secure the preaching of the apostolic gospel for the generations to come, in a context of widespread desertion from it.

## Main themes

There are four major emphases in this letter:

- **Suffering is normal in gospel ministry.** Timothy must be ready to join Paul in suffering for the gospel, for everyone who wants to live a godly life in Christ Jesus will be persecuted. So Christians must not abandon ministers just because they are suffering – they may suffer because they are faithful.

- **Worldly church leaders will undermine faithful gospel ministry.** Their godless chatter that leads to ungodliness will spread like gangrene. It will sound like godliness but will lack any moral power, and it will lead men of depraved minds to oppose the truth. We see this everywhere today.

- **The rewards of faithful gospel ministry are primarily in the life to come.** The gospel is a promise of life and immortality in Christ in the eternal glory and crown of righteousness of the heavenly kingdom. We mustn't expect a comfortable time or the Lord's rewards now, but when He appears with His kingdom.

- **We must keep teaching the apostolic gospel of Christ.** We must testify about our Lord, keep Paul's teaching as our pattern, entrust it to others who will be able faithfully to teach it, keep reminding others of it, correctly handle the Word of truth, gently instruct opponents, and preach the Word whether or not it's popular and whether or not we feel like it, correcting, rebuking and encouraging with great patience and careful instruction.

The following two great charges summarise the letter: 'Do not be ashamed to testify about our Lord, or ashamed of me his prisoner. But join with me in suffering for the gospel, by the power of God' (1 v 8); and 'In the presence of God and of Christ Jesus, who will judge the living and the dead, and in view of his appearing and his kingdom, I give you this charge: Preach the Word' (4 v 1-2).

## Onesiphorus

Onesiphorus is an important example for Timothy and all Christians today, not just because he was a faithful friend and helpful man. His loyalty to Paul was an expression of his loyalty to Paul's gospel. He is an example of remaining faithful both to sound teaching and to the sound teachers who must proclaim it. When bishops and leaders are abandoning the gospel everywhere, it will be faithful church members who preserve the gospel for the next generation in this country – loyal men like Onesiphorus.

## Questions for group discussion

1. How can we refresh those who preach the gospel?

2. How can we avoid being ashamed of the gospel and those who preach it?

3. How can we help those in gospel ministry?

4. How could we support those imprisoned for their Christian faith?

# CONCLUSION: JESUS – THE PERFECT MAN

**W**e may have many heroes, but who is the superhero? Who is the one who stands head and shoulders above the rest? We may support a football team, but there'll be one player we admire above all, a John Terry, a Thierry Henry, a Wayne Rooney or a Steven Gerrard.

When the BBC conducted its poll for the top ten Britons of the last millennium, there was one who rose above Cromwell, Newton and Brunel: the bulldog himself, Winston Churchill. Rightly, he towered above them all. Likewise, the Bible offers many heroes for Christians to admire and emulate. I've selected just a few good men. But towering over them all, the Colossus looking down on midgets, the superhero among mere mortals, is the Lord Jesus Himself. He is not just one of 'a few good men', He is the perfect man, the real man, the only God-Man. God's Word urges Christian men consciously to enthrone Jesus as the super-hero we admire, follow and love.

The Bible is all about Jesus. Jesus said of the Old Testament: 'These are the Scriptures that testify about me' (John 5 v 39). The risen Jesus turned to the same Scriptures to explain His own death and resurrection: 'Everything must be fulfilled that is written about me in the Law of Moses, the Prophets and the Psalms' (Luke 24 v 44). The Scriptures are described by Paul as 'able to make you wise for salvation through faith in Christ Jesus' (2 Timothy 3 v 15).

Not that every sentence, verse or paragraph is about Jesus; they may be about Satan, sin or Jerusalem. They may not specifically mention Jesus. But every sentence, verse and paragraph is related to the gospel of Jesus as the background for understanding Him. If we can't relate a passage to Jesus, we haven't yet understood it.

Historical figures in Scripture may relate to Jesus in a number of ways. Some figures are largely historical background, eg: which king of Israel came next or which family inherited a particular part of Canaan (even then, all kings have to be measured against Christ, and the inheritance in Canaan speaks of our inheritance in heaven!). But some real historical figures had specific roles that could only be perfectly fulfilled by Christ.

Judges, prophets, priests and kings were delegated roles in Israel that awaited the arrival of Jesus. They are described under the direction of God's Spirit so as to enable us to compare them with ideals that can only be true of Christ. Their strengths help us understand the value of Jesus (eg: David's victory over Goliath prefigures Christ's victory over Satan), but their failings cry out for someone better (eg: David's wicked adultery with Bathsheba and murder of Uriah makes us long for a king who is self-controlled and gives life).

It is no surprise, and not fanciful, to discover that the characteristics of 'a few good men' find their perfect expression in the only perfect man. We shall see that Jesus is the ideal combination of all these impressive and lovely graces, and of many more besides.

My purpose is to show you something of how utterly magnificent Jesus is. I want to commend Him to you as your life's inspiring Hero, challenging Master and personal Delight. We will find that Jesus is well worthy of our devotion and worship. Let's consider the virtues of 'a few good men' as each is perfected in Jesus.

## Obedient

Noah was good, but Jesus was perfect.

Noah obediently built an extraordinary boat and stocked it with animals. All His life, Jesus was completely obedient to the will of the Father expressed in both the Old Testament Scriptures and the daily direction of the Holy Spirit. This obedience was most sorely tested on the night before He died. Not only a brutal flogging and agonising crucifixion, but the torment of hellish separation from

His Father lay before Him. He could have rebelled, as we regularly do. He was certainly overcome with trepidation. But he conquered the temptation to disobey the Father in the garden of Gethsemane: 'Going a little farther, he fell to the ground and prayed that if possible the hour might pass from him. "Abba, Father," he said, "everything is possible for you. Take this cup from me. Yet not what I will, but what you will"' (Mark 14 v 35-36). Though everything in Him wanted to avoid the cross, the bottom line, as always, was to obey His Father.

This was not an isolated incident. He explained to His disciples: 'I have obeyed my Father's commands and remain in his love' (John 15 v 10). Looking back over His whole life He could say: 'I have obeyed'. Not just occasionally, or even often, but every single moment of every single day. As a child, teenager and adult, from morning until night, He was obedient. Knowing that the salvation of the world depended upon His perfect obedience, He faced the normal provocations we all face: annoying parental demands, irritating brothers, sisters and school friends, the seductions of wealth, women and wine; but He never strayed for a moment.

Even harder, He faced the appalling indignity of injustice and persecution. Yet, 'Although he was a son, he learned obedience from what he suffered and, once made perfect [lit. *complete*], he became the source of eternal salvation for all who obey him' (Hebrews 5 v 8-9). Though He knew He was God the Son, Designer and Sustainer of everyone He met and everything He saw, He was obedient, even as his creatures bashed and hammered Him.

Noah was relatively obedient, but Jesus was perfectly obedient. Keeping the Ten Commandments? Jesus got ten out of ten every day – the perfect Jewish life! Living according to His own Sermon on the Mount? Jesus observed every detail all the time – the perfect Christian life! We may admire elite soldiers such as those in the SAS for their willingness to obey the most difficult military commands. But no-one would ever try to claim that the SAS are obedient and fearless in their private lives as well. Jesus, however, was completely obedient to the Word of God in all areas of public and private life. He never failed – from His cradle to His grave. He was perfect.

This beautiful and extraordinary devotion to the Father did not only qualify Him for the throne of heaven. His obedience saved His people as well: 'For just as through the disobedience of the one man the many were made sinners, so also through the obedience of the one man the many will be made righteous' (Romans 5 v 19). We are guilty not only for what we do wrong but also for what our ancestor Adam did wrong (because he was the representative of humanity who definitely behaved as each of us would also have done). Adam's disobedience ('original sin') is imputed to us in addition to our own, personal disobedience.

But by God's grace, Jesus is the final Adam and representative of His people, and His daily obedience to every detail of Scripture – even unto death on a cross – is imputed to us and counted as ours. Jesus swapped places with us on the cross. There God treated Jesus as if he were us (disobedient) and punished Him. Now He treats us as if we were Jesus (obedient) and accepts us. How wonderful is that! Jesus' perfect obedience is our obedience, our qualification for heaven! *Admire Him!*

### Sacrificial

Abraham was good, but Jesus was perfect.

Abraham offered his son to die, in confidence that God would raise him. Jesus offered Himself to suffer our death, even though He is the exalted Son of God, and we are hell-deserving enemies of God! Many men have sacrificed themselves for others. Soldiers have died for comrades, lifeboat men have died to save stranded sailors, husbands have died rescuing their wives or children. But I have never heard of a man dying to save dirty maggots, especially maggots that once hated him! Jesus is the exalted Son of Man, the glorious Judge of all the earth. He shouldn't have to stoop to help offensive little creatures like us. He should just crush us underfoot.

Tsar Peter the Great of Russia is admired for humbling himself to work in disguise among the dockers of a Russian port so that he could understand and help his people. By comparison, the Son of God dying for us is, surely, like us dying for the maggots in the bottom of a rotting dustbin. Yet He said: 'For even the Son of Man did not come to be served, but to serve, and to give his life as a ransom for many' (Mark 10 v 45).

Jesus must have found the competition for glory between His disciples absolutely pathetic (just as our own competitive desire for status and honour in ministry is still pathetic). He is our Creator, Saviour and Lord, our Prophet, Priest and King, yet He offered Himself to suffer as the ransom price for our eternal freedom! And he succeeded: 'But now he has appeared once for all at the end of the ages to do away with sin by the sacrifice of himself' (Hebrews 9 v 26). He has done away forever with the condemnation and power of sin. And He has therefore satisfied the Father and reconciled Him to us: 'For there is one God and one mediator between God and men, the man Christ Jesus, who gave himself as a ransom for all men' (1 Timothy 2 v 5-6).

Abraham was relatively sacrificial, but Jesus was perfectly so. He gave up everything for us, who are offensive in our sin, out of passionate love for the Father and for us. Nothing we ever give up will ever remotely come close to what it cost Jesus to ransom us for His family in heaven. *Thank Him!*

## Self-disciplined
Joseph was good, but Jesus was perfect.

Joseph resisted the seduction of Mrs Potiphar, but Jesus resisted the sustained assaults of Satan with far more reasonable temptations:

> Then Jesus was led by the Spirit into the desert to be tempted by the devil. After fasting for forty days and forty nights, he was hungry. The tempter came to him and said, 'If you are the Son of God, tell these stones to become bread.'

> Jesus answered, 'It is written: "Man does not live on bread alone, but on every word that comes from the mouth of God"... '
> **Matthew 4 v 1-4**

Satan's temptation for the starving Jesus was to reject the Word of God momentarily, briefly abandon His mission of accepting the constraints of our human life (so as to qualify for suffering the penalty of our sin on the cross), and to use His divine status for His own benefit. Adam had surrendered to Satan's temptation to disobey God. He ate the forbidden fruit in the Garden of Eden. Israel had been in the desert for forty years. When hungry they rebelled against God. But on behalf of the human race and Israel, Jesus succeeded where Adam and the wilderness Israelites failed.

Quoting from Moses' description in Deuteronomy of Israel's testing, Jesus remained faithful and obedient to God's Word. Here was the perfect founder of new humanity and the new people of God. We rightly admire Nelson Mandela for his restraint when released from prison in not seeking vengeance. Other men have been self-controlled with money, sex or power. But only Christ has been perfectly self-disciplined in all areas of life all of the time. By this self-discipline, Jesus remained qualified as our perfect Saviour who could die for the sins of others. But his self-discipline has greater significance still.

'Because he himself suffered when he was tempted, he is able to help those who are being tempted' (Hebrews 2 v 18). We are bombarded every day with the temptations of Satan and of our own sinful natures. We have little idea how to resist. He knows exactly what we need to do. He can help us with the instructions of His Word and the power of His Spirit. He can strengthen us to tackle the temptations we face.

And we can be sure that He is willing to do so:

> For we do not have a high priest who is unable to sympathise with our weaknesses, but we have one who has been tempted in every way, just as we are – yet was without sin. Let us then approach the

> throne of grace with confidence, so that we may receive mercy and
> find grace to help us in our time of need.     **Hebrews 4 v 15-16**

Jesus has felt the full strength of temptation (after all, temptations constantly resisted become more powerful than those to which we surrender). He does know, from personal experience, what temptation to envy, lust or greed feels like. He is sympathetic to our condition. So we can approach Him both for mercy and forgiveness for our failures, and for grace and strength to resist. Faced with fierce temptation to sin, our only hope of resistance is to pray to Jesus. Weak and hesitant perhaps at first, we gather strength from Him as we keep calling upon Him for help.

Joseph was impressive in resisting sex with Mrs Potiphar, but Jesus has resisted every kind of sin, permanently. *Learn from Him!*

## Unworldly

Moses was good, but Jesus was perfect.

Moses grew up in the luxury of an Egyptian palace and gave it up to join Israel. God the Son had eternally lived in the glory and delight of the love of God in heavenly paradise, and gave it up for the cross! It is very remarkable to see what kind of life God chose for Himself when He took flesh in Mary's womb: 'Then a teacher of the law came to him and said, "Teacher, I will follow you wherever you go." Jesus replied, "Foxes have holes and birds of the air have nests, but the Son of Man has nowhere to lay his head"' (Matthew 8 v 19-20).

Where we might have allowed ourselves some modest middle-class privileges, God Himself was born out of wedlock in a cattle shed. His family were then hunted refugees in Egypt before returning to the provincial backwater of Nazareth. There, Jesus learned Joseph's trade in a large and unimpressive family. When He embarked upon His mission publicly, He became a wandering preacher. But He didn't seek the financial patronage that many nurtured. What is especially striking is that He didn't even secure the kind of church building and accommodation that we would think was necessary for pastoral ministry. He remained a poor travelling teacher.

One imagines that a lucrative ministry of healing was open to Him. He could have lived well from those who were grateful for His help. But God the Son chose to live with a very lowly standard of living. We rightly admire men like Eric Liddell, who gave up the benefits of Olympic success, and then travelled to reach the people of China with the gospel. But Christ is the King of kings, who gave up the glory of heaven for the road to the cross.

He was not ascetic – He enjoyed weddings and festive meals. He didn't walk the sacrificial way of the cross because He was masochistic but in order to save us. His poverty reached its desperate depth as He hung, wracked with pain, humiliated, presumably naked, mocked and hated, under the curse of God upon a Roman gibbet. Yet, by His poverty, we have been given every spiritual blessing in Him, in the heavenly realms, awaiting our arrival. 'For you know the grace of our Lord Jesus Christ, that though he was rich, yet for your sakes he became poor, so that you through his poverty might become rich' (2 Corinthians 8 v 9).

Moses was impressively unworldly, but only Jesus gave up heaven for the poverty of the cross. *Emulate Him!*

### Wholehearted

Caleb was good, but Jesus was perfect.

Caleb maintained confidence in God even against threatening opposition, but Jesus was to face the powers of Satan himself on the cross. We read that, while His disciples were filled with trepidation, Jesus walked straight into the lion's mouth, dragging His followers with Him: 'They were on their way up to Jerusalem, with Jesus leading the way, and the disciples were astonished, while those who followed were afraid. Again he took the Twelve aside and told them what was going to happen to him' (Mark 10 v 32). Jesus knew exactly what was to come. He had read Psalm 22 (He would quote from it on the cross). He knew the appalling suffering ahead of Him. Yet He resolutely surrendered Himself to capture.

When he stood before the Sanhedrin council on trumped-up charges, Jesus refused to defend Himself and freely confessed who He was, knowing the implications:

> The high priest said to him, 'I charge you under oath by the living God: Tell us if you are the Christ, the Son of God.'
>
> 'Yes, it is as you say,' Jesus replied. 'But I say to all of you: In the future you will see the Son of Man sitting at the right hand of the Mighty One and coming on the clouds of heaven.'
>
> Then the high priest tore his clothes and said, 'He has spoken blasphemy! Why do we need any more witnesses? Look, now you have heard the blasphemy. What do you think?'
>
> 'He is worthy of death,' they answered'. **Matthew 26 v 63-66**

Jesus trusted that, beyond His suffering, He would arrive in heaven upon the clouds of glory to take His seat beside the Father and judge the world. His faith in God's promises in Scripture remained absolutely rock solid, even as He endured the hostile hatred of His enemies alone.

We rightly admire Martin Luther for courageously confronting the power of the Pope and the mediaeval Roman Catholic Church in proclaiming justification 'by faith alone in Christ alone'. In 1521, on trial for his life, in the speech that shook the world he declared: 'My conscience is captive to the Word of God. It is unsafe and dangerous to do anything against one's conscience. Here I stand; I cannot do otherwise. So help me God.' But this was new for Luther. He hadn't been wholehearted all his life as Jesus was.

Caleb showed courage on the basis of God's word in his willingness to wait and then fight for his inheritance. Jesus demonstrated perfect faith and courage in the Father as He accepted the torture of floggings, impalement and hell. Therefore:

> Let us fix our eyes on Jesus, the author and perfecter of our faith, who for the joy set before him endured the cross, scorning its shame, and sat down at the right hand of the throne of God. Consider him who endured such opposition from sinful men, so that you will not grow weary and lose heart'. **Hebrews 12 v 2-3**

Considering what Christ endured, we can wait and not grow weary. We can fight and not lose heart, in wholehearted confidence that God will keep His promise. *Consider Him!*

## Humble

Isaiah was good, but Jesus was perfect.

Isaiah was humbled by the holiness of God to recognise his sinfulness. Jesus had no sin about which to feel bad, yet He humbled Himself completely under the will of His Father and the needs of His people. Considering that Jesus is God the Son, His gentle humility is extraordinary and no doubt the reason why many people cannot recognise who He really is:

> 'Come to me, all you who are weary and burdened, and I will give you rest. Take my yoke upon you and learn from me, for I am gentle and humble in heart, and you will find rest for your souls.'
> **Matthew 11 v 28-30**

His humility was not a false self-deprecation that denied His divine supremacy, but rather a concern to put the needs of others before His own.

It was Jesus' humility that caused the Father to exalt Him to the highest honour:

> Your attitude should be the same as that of Christ Jesus:
> Who, being in very nature God,
> did not consider equality with God something to be grasped,
> but made himself nothing, taking the very nature of a servant,
> being made in human likeness.
>
> And being found in appearance as a man,
> he humbled himself
> and became obedient to death – even death on a cross!

> Therefore God exalted him to the highest place
> and gave him the name that is above every name ...
>
> **Philippians 2 v 5-9**

Christ descended from the glory of heaven to become fully human, with all our frailty. Then He became our slave, in order to attend to our deepest need of forgiveness. Then he accepted the abject humiliation of a brutal crucifixion. God is not impressed by the brash self-flaunting arrogance of our celebrity culture. He prizes self-denying attention to the needs of others. In Jesus, this was perfect. We rightly admire men like Ronald Wilcox, a Jute trader in the city of London, who generously established The Good Shepherd Mission – a club for disadvantaged youth in the East End. He regularly attended the club and tirelessly supported its work for the rest of his life. But such humble service cannot compare with the God of glory dying as a mutilated criminal for us.

Indeed, this humility wasn't a short-term submission, but characteristic of all His life: 'During the days of Jesus' life on earth, he offered up prayers and petitions with loud cries and tears to the one who could save him from death, and he was heard because of his reverent submission' (Hebrews 5 v 7).

Isaiah was humbled by God, for he was a man of unclean lips. God the Son humbled Himself to serve us. *Bow before Him!*

## Distinctive

Daniel was good, but Jesus was perfect.

Daniel resolved not to defile himself with any further compromise, so as to remain distinctive as a man of God. Jesus wasn't just different. He was unique. We sometimes domesticate Jesus, imagining Him as a very nice man, a powerful healer and an inspiring teacher. But Jesus was utterly amazing: no one had seen or heard of anyone remotely like Him! This man threw the whole country into turmoil, and the crowds travelled from far and wide to hear Him. He was 'out of this world', we might say.

> The people were all so amazed that they asked each other, 'What is this? A new teaching – and with authority! He even gives orders to evil spirits and they obey him.' News about him spread quickly over the whole region of Galilee...

> He said to the paralytic, 'I tell you, get up, take your mat and go home.' He got up, took his mat and walked out in full view of them all. This amazed everyone and they praised God, saying, 'We have never seen anything like this!'

> He got up, rebuked the wind and said to the waves, 'Quiet! Be still!' Then the wind died down and it was completely calm. He said to his disciples, 'Why are you so afraid? Do you still have no faith?' They were terrified and asked each other, 'Who is this? Even the wind and the waves obey him!' **Mark 1 v 27-28; 2 v 10-12; 4 v 39-41**

It was truly fantastic and frightening to be around Jesus. He exorcised demons and brought light from the Scriptures. He healed the paralysed and raised the dead. He calmed the storms and walked on water. He had unique authority over Satan, sickness and death, as only God could have.

We rightly celebrate the willingness of Wilberforce and others to stand against the power of the slave trade in the Parliament of this land. Wilberforce was relatively distinctive, but he wasn't unique like Jesus. When you sat with Jesus for lunch, you ate with the living God. When Jesus turned to talk to you, you heard the voice of God. When you watched Jesus play with children, you were watching the living God. He wasn't just distinctive, unusual or even special, He was absolutely, life-transformingly magnificent. For:

> He is the image of the invisible God, the firstborn over all creation. For by him all things were created: things in heaven and on earth, visible and invisible, whether thrones or powers or rulers or authorities; all things were created by him and for him. He is before all things, and in him all things hold together. And he is the head of the body, the church; he is the beginning and the firstborn from among the dead, so that in everything he might have the supremacy.
>
> **Colossians 1 v 15-18**

Daniel was impressively distinctive, but Jesus was from another world. *Worship Him!*

## Pastoral

Paul was good, but Jesus was perfect.

Jesus is the Shepherd and Pastor who has served us by laying down His life for us on the cross (John 10). Jesus is the Shepherd and Pastor who has taught us by His apostolic witnesses through the Scriptures (Mark 6). When God promised (Ezekiel 34) to come and search, rescue and gather His sheep (evangelism), to feed, nurture and heal His sheep (discipling) and to judge, defend and rule His sheep (governing), we find Jesus fulfilling these promises and explaining His ministry in the words of the parable of the lost sheep: 'Rejoice with me; I have found my lost sheep' (Luke 15 v 6).

We rightly honour church pastors who have faithfully taught us the gospel, guarded us from error and given us God's word as Paul instructed the Ephesian elders (Acts 20). We respect great pastors like Martin Lloyd-Jones, John Stott, Dick Lucas and Philip Jensen who have taught us to understand each portion of Scripture in its context of sound doctrine, plain meaning, literary theme and biblical theology, respectively. But each of them would acknowledge that they are but 'sheepdogs', driving us to that 'great Shepherd of the sheep' (Hebrews 13 v 20), who is Jesus.

Paul was an outstanding example of pastoral ministry—planting churches for Christ all over the Middle East. But Christ remains the foundation cornerstone of every single church, and He is 'the Chief Shepherd', to whom all other pastors are accountable. *Honour Him!*

## Prayerful

Epaphras was good, but Jesus was perfect. Epaphras prayed for the churches he pastored, but Jesus still prays for them all. Jesus was evidently a man of very considerable prayer: 'Jesus often withdrew to lonely places and prayed' (Luke 5 v 16). Not only did Jesus maintain the Jewish disciplines of prayer, praying the Shema (from Deuteronomy 6) and some version of the 'Eighteen Benedictions' (the main prayers of the synagogue at the time[1]) three times a day, in addition to prayer in the synagogue on Saturday. But, clearly, He also prayed often in secret (as He recommended to us in the Sermon on the Mount) so as not to pray for public approval, and especially at times of crisis and decision. Jesus communed intimately with His Father in prayer, seeking His strength and guidance for what lay ahead.

But it is not just the fact that He prayed, but also the manner of His praying from which we must learn: 'During the days of Jesus' life on earth, he offered up prayers and petitions with loud cries and tears to the one who could save him from death' (Hebrews 5 v 7). Jesus wrestled in prayer.

Indeed Jesus has never stopped praying. We rightly admire godly men like Robert Murray McCheyne, who spent the first hours of every day in prayer. But even now, at this very moment, Jesus continues to pray, not just for a few Christians, but for every single one of us. 'Christ Jesus, who died – more than that, who was raised to life – is at the right hand of God and is also interceding for us' (Romans 8 v 34).

Ephaphras wrestled in prayer for others to stand firm in Christ. Jesus continues to intercede for all Christians everywhere, praying to the Father for us. *Love Him!*

## Loyal

Onesiphorus was good, but Jesus was perfect. Onesiphorus searched diligently to find Paul and support him. Jesus doesn't have to search for us because His Spirit is always with us. His final instructions to His disciples are famously known as His 'Great Commission'. He claimed all authority over the world; He commanded that disciples be made of all nations; and He promised to be with us at all times:

> Then Jesus came to them and said, 'All authority in heaven and on earth has been given to me. Therefore go and make disciples of all nations, baptising them in the name of the Father and of the Son and of the Holy Spirit, and teaching them to obey everything I have commanded you. And surely I am with you always, to the very end of the age'.
> **Matthew 28 v 18-20**

His reference to the end of the age makes it clear that He had in mind not only the disciples he was speaking to, but also the generations of disciples coming after them. The Spirit of Christ is always with us as we go about His mission in His world. He is grieved by our sin, assures and instructs us by His Word, and empowers us to remain faithful. He is with us now to provide, pardon and protect.

Paul recalled that, when everyone else had deserted him, the Lord was with him: 'At my first defence, no one came to my support, but everyone deserted me. May it not be held against them. But the Lord stood at my side and gave me strength' (2 Timothy 4 v 16-17). Christians today, under pressure in the office or at the club, in the home or in the pub, will find that the Lord stands by us when we're in need of help. We rightly admire agencies like Christian Solidarity Worldwide, the Barnabas Fund or Release International for their ministry to persecuted believers. But the Spirit of Christ is with every believer in every courtroom and prison, in every threatened difficulty, in every country in the world. The Lord is always with us. *Rely on Him!*

These 'Few good men' are really an identikit, photofit, CV and advertisement for Jesus. Jesus remains as obedient, sacrificial, self-disciplined, unworldly, whole-hearted, humble, distinctive, pastoral, prayerful and loyal today in heaven, as He was when He lived on earth. We must not only worship and admire Him passionately, follow and emulate Him carefully, commend and proclaim Him boldly, but also look forward to being with Him joyfully.

### *References*

1 See W. D. Davies, The Setting of the Sermon on the Mount, CUP, 1963.